the   cial

AN INTRODUCTION TO THE SOCIAL SCIENCES: UNDERSTANDING SOCIAL CHANGE

This book is part of a series produced in association with The Open University. The complete list of books in the series is as follows:

Questioning Identity: Gender, Class, Nation
edited by Kath Woodward

The Natural and the Social: Uncertainty, Risk, Change
edited by Steve Hinchliffe and Kath Woodward

Ordering Lives: Family, Work and Welfare
edited by Gordon Hughes and Ross Fergusson

A Globalizing World? Culture, Economics, Politics
edited by David Held

Knowledge and the Social Sciences: Theory, Method, Practice
edited by David Goldblatt

The books form part of the Open University course DD100 *An Introduction to the Social Sciences: Understanding Social Change*. Details of this and other Open University courses can be obtained from the Course Reservations Centre, PO Box 724, The Open University, Milton Keynes MK7 6ZS, United Kingdom: tel. +44 (0)1908 653231, e-mail ces-gen@open.ac.uk

Alternatively, you may visit the Open University website at http://www.open.ac.uk where you can learn more about the wide range of courses and packs offered at all levels by The Open University.

For availability of other course components, contact Open University Worldwide Ltd, The Berrill Building, Walton Hall, Milton Keynes MK7 6AA, United Kingdom: tel. +44 (0)1908 858785; fax +44 (0)1908 858787; e-mail ouwenq@open.ac.uk; website http://www.ouw.co.uk

the natural and the social: uncertainty, risk, change

edited by steve hinchliffe and kath woodward

London and New York

in association with

The Open University

11954639

Learning Resources
Centre

First published 2000 by Routledge; written and produced by The Open University
11 New Fetter Lane, London EC4P 4EE

Simultaneously published in the USA and Canada by Routledge
29 West 35th Street, New York, NY 10001

Routledge is an imprint of the Taylor & Francis Group

This text has been printed on paper produced in Sweden from wood from managed forests using an elemental chlorine-free bleaching process. It has been stated as being environmentally friendly by the Swedish Association for the Protection of Nature.

Edited, designed and typeset by The Open University.

Printed by The Bath Press, Bath.

British Library Cataloguing in Publication Data
A catalogue record for this book is available from The British Library

Library of Congress Cataloging in Publication Data
A catalogue record for this book has been requested

ISBN 0-415-22289-3 (hbk)

ISBN 0-415-22290-7 (pbk)

1.1

Contents

Series preface   vii

Introduction   1
Steve Hinchliffe

CHAPTER 1
Human nature   7
Steve Hinchliffe and Judith Greene

CHAPTER 2
Whose health is it anyway?   43
Brenda Smith and David Goldblatt

CHAPTER 3
Nature for sale   79
Susan Himmelweit and Roberto Simonetti

CHAPTER 4
Living with risk: the unnatural geography of environmental
crises   117
Steve Hinchliffe

Afterword   155
Steve Hinchliffe

Acknowledgements   161

Index   163

The Open University course team

John Allen, *Senior Lecturer in Geography*

Penny Bennett, *Editor*

Pam Berry, *Compositor*

Simon Bromley, *Senior Lecturer in Government*

David Calderwood, *Project Controller*

Elizabeth Chaplin, *Tutor Panel*

Giles Clark, *Co-publishing Advisor*

Stephen Clift, *Editor*

Allan Cochrane, *Professor of Public Policy*

Lene Connolly, *Print Buying Controller*

Graham Dawson, *Lecturer in Economics*

Lesley Duguid, *Senior Course Co-ordination Secretary*

Ross Fergusson, *Staff Tutor in Social Policy*

Fran Ford, *Senior Course Co-ordination Secretary*

David Goldblatt, *Co-Course Team Chair, Lecturer in Government*

Jenny Gove, *Lecturer in Psychology*

Judith Greene, *Professor of Psychology*

Montserrat Guibernau, *Lecturer in Government*

Peter Hamilton, *Lecturer in Sociology*

Celia Hart, *Picture Researcher*

David Held, *Professor of Politics and Sociology*

Susan Himmelweit, *Senior Lecturer in Economics*

Steve Hinchliffe, *Lecturer in Geography*

Gordon Hughes, *Lecturer in Social Policy*

Christina Janoszka, *Course Manager*

Pat Jess, *Staff Tutor in Geography*

Bob Kelly, *Staff Tutor in Government*

Margaret Kiloh, *Staff Tutor in Applied Social Sciences*

Sylvia Lay-Flurrie, *Secretary*

Siân Lewis, *Graphic Designer*

Tony McGrew, *Professor of International Relations, University of Southampton*

Hugh Mackay, *Staff Tutor in Sociology*

Maureen Mackintosh, *Professor of Economics*

Eugene McLaughlin, *Senior Lecturer in Applied Social Science*

Andrew Metcalf, *Senior Producer, BBC*

Gerry Mooney, *Staff Tutor in Applied Social Sciences*

Ray Munns, *Graphic Artist*

Kathy Pain, *Staff Tutor in Geography*

Clive Pearson, *Tutor Panel*

Lynne Poole, *Tutor Panel*

Norma Sherratt, *Staff Tutor in Sociology*

Roberto Simonetti, *Lecturer in Economics*

Dick Skellington, *Project Officer*

Brenda Smith, *Staff Tutor in Psychology*

Mark Smith, *Lecturer in Social Sciences*

Grahame Thompson, *Professor of Political Economy*

Ken Thompson, *Professor of Sociology*

Stuart Watt, *Lecturer in Psychology/KMI*

Andy Whitehead, *Graphic Artist*

Kath Woodward, *Co-Course Team Chair, Staff Tutor in Sociology*

Chris Wooldridge, *Editor*

External Assessor

Nigel Thrift, *Professor of Geography, University of Bristol*

Series preface

The Natural and the Social: Uncertainty, Risk, Change is the second in a series of five books, entitled *An Introduction to the Social Sciences: Understanding Social Change*. If the social sciences are to retain and extend their relevance in the twenty-first century there can be little doubt that they will have to help us understand social change. In the 1990s an introductory course to the social sciences would have looked completely different.

From a global perspective it appears that the pace of change is quickening, social and political ideas and institutions are under threat. The international landscape has changed; an intensification of technological change across computing, telecommunications, genetics and biotechnology present new political, cultural and moral dilemmas and opportunities. Real intimations of a global environmental crisis in the making have emerged. We are, it appears, living in an uncertain world. We are in new territory.

The same is also true of more local concerns. At the beginning of the twenty-first century both societies and the social sciences are in a state of flux. *Understanding Social Change* has been written at a moment that reflects, albeit in a partial way, subterranean shifts in the social and cultural character of the UK. Established social divisions and social identities of class, gender, ethnicity and nation are fragmenting and re-forming. Core institutions such as the family, work and welfare have become more diverse and complex. It is also a moment when significant processes of change have been set in train – such as constitutional reform and European economic and monetary union – whose longer-term trajectory remains uncertain. The flux in the social sciences has been tumultuous. Social change, uncertainty and diversity have rendered many of the most well-established frameworks in the social sciences of limited use and value. Social change on this scale demands fresh perspectives and new systems of explanation.

In this context *Understanding Social Change* is part of a bold and innovative educational project, for it attempts to capture and explore these processes of momentous social change and in doing so reasserts the utility and necessity of the social sciences. Each of the five books which make up the series attempts precisely this, and they all do so from a fundamentally interdisciplinary perspective. Social change is no respecter of the boundaries of disciplines and the tidy boxes that social scientists have often tried to squeeze it into. Above all, *Understanding Social Change* seeks to maintain and extend the Open University's democratic educational mission: to reach and enthuse an enormously diverse student population; to insist that critical, informed, reflexive engagement with the direction of social change is not a matter for elites and professional social scientists alone.

As you may have guessed, this series of books forms a core component of the Open University, Faculty of Social Sciences, level 1 course, DD100 *An Introduction to the Social Sciences: Understanding Social Change*. Each book in the series can be read independently of the other books and independently from the rest of the materials that make up the Open University course. However, if you wish to use the series as a whole, there are a number of references to chapters in other books in the series, and these are easily identifiable because they are printed in bold type.

Making the course and these books has been a long and complex process, and thanks are due to an enormous number of people.

First and foremost, the entire project has been managed and kept on the rails, when it was in mortal danger of flying off them, by our excellent Course Manager, Christina Janoszka. In the DD100 office, Fran Ford, Lesley Duguid and Sylvia Lay-Flurrie have been the calm eye at the centre of a turbulent storm, our thanks to all of them.

Stephen Clift, Chris Wooldridge and Penny Bennett have been meticulous, hawk-eyed editors. Siân Lewis has provided superb design work, and Ray Munns and Andy Whitehead have provided skilled cartographic and artistic work. David Calderwood in project control has arranged and guided the schedule with calm efficiency and Celia Hart has provided great support with illustrations and photographs. Nigel Thrift, our external assessor, and Clive Pearson, Elizabeth Chaplin and Lynne Poole, our tutor panel, have provided consistent and focused criticism, support and advice. Peggotty Graham has been an invaluable friend of *Understanding Social Change* and David Held has provided balance, perspective and insight as only he can.

It only remains for us to say that we hope you find *Understanding Social Change* an engaging and illuminating introduction to the social sciences, and in turn you find the social sciences essential for understanding life in the twenty-first century.

David Goldblatt
Kath Woodward
Co-Chairs, The Open University Course Team

Introduction

Steve Hinchliffe

This book is about the ways in which society and nature combine. You may be used to thinking that society and nature, almost by definition, are matters to be kept apart. Indeed, in our everyday language, we tend to treat nature and society as opposites. If something is described as natural, then we tend to think that it is unlikely to have much to do with society. So, for example, when we describe a landscape as 'natural' we often mean to suggest that it is undeveloped, untouched and that the social world is largely absent. When we talk about someone having a natural talent (for music or sport, say), then we tend to imply that they were born with it. The social worlds of education and training are almost thought to be irrelevant to the way in which we judge their particular 'gift'.

To think like this is to think of the social and the natural as separate or pure categories. It is almost as if they are different objects, with neat boundaries and no overlap. We can call this way of thinking about the social and the natural a *purified* approach. Figure 1 is a schematic representation of this purified view.

FIGURE I Nature and society as pure categories

This book sets out to challenge this purified view of nature and society. Each of the chapters deals with different topics, from genetic inheritance and childhood development (Chapter 1), to health care and medicine (Chapter 2), to markets and pollution (Chapter 3), to natural hazards and food scares (Chapter 4). One way of thinking about the book's structure is that we move from 'inner nature' (bodies, organs and personalities) to 'outer nature' (the environments and the non-human world within which we live and co-exist with other people, plants and animals). Common to all the chapters is an attempt to break down the assumed boundaries between nature and society. Indeed, the conviction is that the categories of nature and society are impossible to hold apart when we engage with the real worlds in which people live.

This breaking down of boundaries might seem counter-intuitive. So here are two examples to start you thinking about nature and society interrelationships.

1 Cloning Ryan Giggs

  After a series of bad results, the Welsh football manager joked that he wouldn't mind a clone or two of his star player, Ryan Giggs. Giggs is a player with natural talent, a player with a gift, a player born with a special set of genes. Now, joking apart, what would it mean to really produce an exact replica of Ryan Giggs? Is it simply a matter of taking a few cells from his body, extracting the genetic material and inserting it into an unfertilized egg? If we then transfer this egg into a surrogate mother, will the organism that develops really be another Welsh international footballer? Is there more to him than that?

What about Giggs's upbringing, would that matter? Can we really treat his body and the body of his surrogate mother as pure nature? Will his 'mother's' pregnancy be important? Will she eat the right foods, do the right exercises and get the right treatment? Does the intensive training provided by his football club, Manchester United – one of the richest in the world – matter? If we were truly serious about a Ryan Giggs clone, then wouldn't we have to provide a copy of all or most of his (and his pregnant mother's) interactions with other people, organizations and institutions? In other words, isn't Ryan Giggs a human being who has a social as well as a natural life? (Try not to let your preconceptions about football players or the team you support colour your answer.) In this book we will argue that when we talk about people's identities and lives, it doesn't really make much sense to tease the natural and the social apart.

2   Natural parks?

Now look at the photograph in Figure 2 of Snowdonia National Park. Would you say it was a natural or a social scene? In many ways it looks to be untouched by social worlds. But on closer inspection there are signs that this scene is as social as it is natural.

FIGURE 2   Snowdonia National Park: a natural or a social landscape?

For example, the grasses and peaty soils are the result of thousands of years of human involvement in the land. Much of this land has been deforested in the past two thousand years and used for grazing sheep. If the sheep were removed, under present climatic conditions, the landscape would soon be dominated by scrub. The sheep are domesticated breeds that owe their form to generations of selective breeding. They are not just domesticates (which literally means brought into the house, or we could say 'socialized'), they are also commodities. Their status as marketable products is linked into a whole range of social institutions. These include land and property rights (notice the fence running across the landscape), currency markets, the Ministry of Agriculture, the European Commission, the radiation from the nearby nuclear power station, wholesalers, supermarkets, consumers of lamb meat and wool products, and production and transportation economies that link this scene to places as far away as New Zealand. All of these are tied into the Snowdonia scene in various ways and at various times by virtue of their connection to hill sheep farming. And the connections can shift in ways that can change our 'natural' scene. For example, as financial subsidies to farmers are cut, as dietary habits change and as imports become cheaper, the economics of hill sheep farming in areas like Snowdonia may become more marginal and precarious.

If the economics of hill sheep farming become any more marginal than they already are, then the landscape might change very radically indeed. In order to preserve this scene, the National Park authorities, the National Trust and other organizations will not only have to protect wildlife and vegetation, they will also have to protect the farmers and their livelihoods. To do so, money will need to be raised from elsewhere. The ability to raise money will partly depend on the wider population valuing this scene. In sum, the ecology of this scene not only includes the plants, animals and climate of North Wales, it also includes a wide range of equally changeable social and economic relations.

These examples may have convinced you that nature and society are indeed two sides of the same coin. The following four chapters will contain further examples and issues that should convince you even further. We can now state our first major aim of this book. It is largely inspired by feminist social sciences and more lately by the work of the French sociologist Bruno Latour (1993).

Aim 1: To demonstrate that nature and society are rarely if ever purely natural or purely social. The social and the natural exist in mixes.

However, we won't stop there. The aim of the book is not simply to demonstrate the entangled character of nature and society. Our second aim is to suggest that this demonstration of impurity is both useful and necessary at the current time. As we embark upon a new millennium, we are faced with increasing evidence that our attempts to understand nature and society as pure categories (Figure 1) no longer suits our world. We could not, for example, see an easy way to manage the environment in Snowdonia without understanding something of the nature and society mix that exists in this part of Wales. Nor could we hope to make an informed decision on the implications for human beings of new genetic technologies without understanding the social and natural mix that goes into being human. In short, in this world where risks and uncertainties seem to be piling up on top of one another, we need ways of understanding that refuse to purify the world into nature on the one hand and society on the other. If we are to make improvements to people's lives, not to mention other species' lives, then any attempts to understand nature without society, or to understand society without nature, will prove insufficient to the task. We can now state our second aim.

Aim 2: To demonstrate the importance of considering nature and society together at a point in time when we seem to be faced with ever increasing uncertainty and risk.

The final aim of the book is to demonstrate that the social sciences provide some of the most promising vantage points from where we can start this difficult task of thinking about nature and society as two sides of the same coin. Too often, it seems, environmental and bio-medical questions are left to 'scientific' experts. This is particularly the case in Britain. The result is that we approach nature and society questions by either ignoring society altogether, or by using models of society that are out of date or grossly simplified. This book, therefore, contains a significant amount of work that will introduce you to some of the approaches and techniques that are used in the social sciences. Likewise, the text is written so as to emphasize the ways in which social scientists develop arguments by engaging with different kinds of evidence. So here is our third and final aim.

Aim 3: To demonstrate the resources and skills that social scientists can bring to social and natural issues and debates.

In Chapter 1, Steve Hinchliffe and Judith Greene ask what it means to be a human being, looking at the similarities and differences between and within species. These ideas are developed by focusing on the roles of genetic and social inheritance as ways of understanding children's intelligence and cognitive development. The chapter presents the various arguments for and against natural inheritance and looks at the kinds of evidence used to support researchers' claims. This focus on inner nature continues in Chapter 2 where Brenda Smith and David Goldblatt discuss health and illness. The chapter takes you through various ways in which our bodies and health are understood. Behind each of these is a different understanding of nature and society relations and the authors demonstrate how each has its successes and failures. Through a history of British health policy, Brenda and David also demonstrate how our approach to inner nature and health is bound into particular versions of society. The current emphasis given to lifestyle and risk, which on the face of it sounds as though it manages to integrate social and environmental issues, is linked to a broader move in society to individualize responsibility for health. The integration of environment and society is taken up in Chapter 3, where Sue Himmelweit and Roberto Simonetti discuss the role of markets in the production of environmental degradation. As they are currently organized, markets tend to place no value on large areas of life that we have become used to calling nature. The authors demonstrate in detail why this under-valuing occurs and then critically examine the kinds of policies that economists have devised to deal with the problem. They argue that integrating nature and society may be possible through market adjustments, but we need to be careful to think politically as well as economically when we try to implement these policies. Finally, in Chapter 4, Steve Hinchliffe takes a more explicit look at living with risk. The argument in this chapter is that risk is often intensified when nature and society are considered as separate matters. He argues that the only way to improve our chances and live with risk more effectively is to seek ways of successfully combining nature and society in our understanding and in our practices. Steve Hinchliffe uses examples from around the world, including natural disasters and food scares, to illustrate the argument.

Each chapter develops its own approach to society and nature issues. The result is a breadth of treatments and approaches. Uniquely, we range over a wide territory, not content to limit ourselves to inner nature or to what are more conventionally called environmental questions. We move from genes to planet earth and back again. In doing so we hope to demonstrate the interconnections between these subject matters and between the various social scientific approaches that we take to them.

Reference

Latour, B. (1993) *We Have Never Been Modern*, London, Harvester Wheatsheaf.

Human nature

Steve Hinchliffe and Judith Greene

chapter 1

Contents

1	**Introduction**	**8**
2	**What is human nature?**	**10**
	2.1 The origin of the species	10
	2.2 Evolution and genes	13
3	**Are people different?**	**19**
	3.1 Inheritance of genes	19
	3.2 Studies of twins	20
	3.3 Adoption studies	26
	3.4 Criticisms of twin studies of intelligence	26
4	**How do children develop?**	**28**
	4.1 Similarity and difference	28
	4.2 Piaget's theory of cognitive development	30
	4.3 Stages of intellectual development	32
	4.4 Later studies of children's intelligence	36
5	**Conclusion**	**40**
	References	**41**
	Further reading	**42**

1 INTRODUCTION

This chapter confronts a set of issues that have become especially prominent in recent years. The overarching question is: what does it mean to be a human being? This question has two meanings. First, it asks: what does it mean to be a member of a group called 'human'? What marks that group out? Does this group share a range of similar features? Are these features biological, social or a mixture of both? Second, the question can be read as: what does it take to be a particular human being? We share similarities but we also like to think that we are all different, and unique. What are the bases for our similarities and differences? Are they natural matters, social matters or do we need to consider the social and natural at one and the same time?

These questions are old questions, but at certain times they seem to take on a special poignancy. The present seems to be just one of those moments – for two reasons. First, as the last century came to a close, it seemed to have become more difficult to see human beings as standing outside the natural world. Environmental catastrophes have made us aware of the links and dependencies that bind human beings and being human to other species and environments. We often congratulate ourselves, as a species, on our intelligence, but if this leads to widespread ruin we may in fact have been kidding ourselves all along. As we embark on a new millennium, many people are arguing that it is time to give some thought to what it now means to be a member of a human species in a wider world.

The second reason for addressing the question what it means to be human relates to the increasingly prominent role that is given to our biology, and more specifically to our genes and their DNA, in accounting for our births, lives and deaths. 'It's all in the genes' is a common response to issues as unrelated to one another as our species' war-mongering, altruism, religious organizations, and methods of care. Likewise, individual differences are increasingly explained by referring to our genetic inheritance. Characteristics as diverse as criminal behaviour, gender, health, intelligence, musical talent and so on are increasingly subject to genetic arguments. (For critiques of genetic explanations for criminality and gender, see Mooney *et al.*, 2000 and **Gove and Watt, 2000** respectively.) What is frightening is that these explanations are becoming so popular that they are starting to have consequences. As the technology to 'read' our genetic 'make up' progresses, it has become more than a possibility that this information will be available to potential employers, health insurers, even to sexual partners. If these people believe that your character, health and so on can be read off from your genetic code, then they may use it to decide whether or not you are worthy of their business. Their assumption would be that you have a biologically determined, and therefore fixed, identity; that is, you are what you are. There is no room for change. Your identity is fixed before you have even done anything (see **Woodward, 2000** for a more dynamic notion of identity). This questionable approach to identity may yield a form of 'knowledge' that can even be used to decide whether or not people should be born in the first place. It is worrying that people are even beginning to talk about 'designer babies'. As the feminist science critic Hilary Rose (1998, p.84) suggests, 'while tasteless, absurd, even impossible, the dream of the perfect baby takes its place alongside other consumer fantasies, of the perfect house, suit, job, garden, partner, etc.'

Part of the reason for this new growth in theories that suggest that our identities are determined by our inner nature or biological structure is due to a relatively recent preoccupation with the science of genetics and with genes. The word 'gene' simply derives from 'genesis', the beginning. Genes are treated by some as the root or beginning and therefore the explanation or cause of everything else (from our birth, to our growth, to our demise). As we shall see, for social scientists, this explanation of human being is far too biological. Interestingly, a number of biologists also reject the idea that life can be understood in terms of genes determining how we or any other member of any other species act (see, for example, Lewontin, 1993). Given the use to which genetic explanations are being put, it is crucial that we clearly demonstrate what else is at stake when it comes to being human. To do this we need to look at the ways in which biology *and* society interact to produce the human species and individual differences within that species.

Three major themes run throughout this chapter. The *first theme* focuses on this issue of human being (or being human). We investigate some of the similarities and differences between and within species. In Section 2 we look at evolutionary explanations of species identity. Sections 3 and 4 focus upon intelligence as an issue that allows us to develop an understanding of the natural and social interactions that go to produce a 'specific species', and variation within a species. The argument will be that, far from intelligence being solely a matter of genes, or of any other aspect of our inner nature, it is the interrelationships between what we have inherited from our parents and all manner of environmental and social interactions that produce differences in intelligence.

The *second theme* is a focus upon the mechanisms and processes that result in similarity and difference within the human species. We will be concerned to demonstrate the ways in which our social and biological lives interact (so much so that it becomes futile to tell them apart). We do this by drawing upon a number of case studies that have been important in social science thinking. In Section 2, we start this discussion by looking at ideas of change over time (evolution). In the two following sections we look at studies of identical and non-identical twins (Section 3) and childhood learning and development (Section 4). The aim in the first case is to review some of the ways in which children who have inherited the same genetic material from their parents can develop striking differences as well as similarities. In the childhood development section, the aim will be to understand the roles of natural and social interactions in producing similarities and differences in the ways in which children learn.

Our *third theme* in this chapter is concerned with social science investigation. We shall be looking at the kinds of methods and evidence that social scientists use to study human attributes and the processes that produce those characteristics. In particular, we will be concerned to demonstrate the role of evidence in building up arguments and making claims.

2 WHAT IS HUMAN NATURE?

This section has two aims. The first aim is to explore the processes that are thought to go into the production of a separate species. The second is to open up some ideas on the processes that produce differences within a species. In both cases, the suggestion is that it is unsatisfactory to give precedence to inner nature, outer nature or to society in explanations of species being. Rather, we need to see these categories as fully entwined in order to understand species differentiation. (The term 'species being' was coined by Karl Marx, and is used here to describe the characteristics, the similarities and differences, that exist within any one species grouping. As we shall see, species being is explained in various ways by biologists and social scientists.)

2.1 The origin of the species

Evolution
Change over time. The evolution of a species is thought by followers of Darwin to occur through natural selection.

We would probably have answered the question 'where do we come from?' very differently two hundred years ago. At that time, human beings and all the other species that inhabit the earth were generally thought to have been placed there by a supernatural power at the creation. After this beginning, or genesis, everything stayed pretty much the same. In terms of longevity, this theory of species form and being was powerful. It lasted for much longer than most theories do today. But, during the eighteenth and nineteenth centuries the theory started to creak under the weight of new evidence and argument. The most famous evidence was that of the fossil record, which showed not only that species come and go – they appear in the record and then become extinct at various times – but also suggested that species' forms changed over time. In other words, far from being fixed, the worlds of plants and animals (and, it was increasingly being argued, that of humans) were dynamic and changing. The word that captured these ideas of a changing world was **evolution**. It simply means change over time.

The most famous name associated with evolutionary thinking is Charles Darwin. In 1859, after many years of travelling, fossil hunting, observing, thinking and collecting evidence, Darwin published *The Origin of Species by Means of Natural Selection*. The idea of evolution was not in itself new, but Darwin was the one who managed not only to *describe what* was happening (changes in species' form over time), but also offered a convincing *explanation* of *how* it was happening (processes and mechanisms).

According to Darwin, evolution occurred as a result of the interactions between members of a species and their environment. As the word interaction suggests, this was a two-way relationship. As the environment changed, so pressures were placed on a species to change accordingly. Similarly, although less often emphasized in subsequent accounts of Darwin's work, as species changed, so their environment would be under pressure to change.

FIGURE 1.1 Charles Darwin

ACTIVITY 1.1

Read Darwin's account of evolutionary pressures below, and answer the following questions:

1 What causes change to occur in the wolf species' being?

2 What do you think will happen subsequently to the wolves' environment (in particular, the other species that it shares its habitat with)?

3 From your own knowledge of dog behaviour, what other characteristic of wolf behaviour might alter this account of change?

> Let us take the case of a wolf, which preys on various animals, securing some by craft, some by strength, and some by fleetness; and let us suppose that the fleetest prey, a deer for instance, had from any change in the country increased in numbers, or that other prey had decreased in numbers, during that season of the year when the wolf is hardest pressed for food. I can under such circumstances see no reason to doubt that the swiftest and slimmest wolves would have the best chance of surviving, and so be preserved or selected, provided always that they retained strength to master their prey at this or at some other period of the year, when they might be compelled to prey on other animals. I can see no more reason to doubt this, than that man [sic] can improve the fleetness of his greyhounds by careful and methodical selection, or by that unconscious selection which results from each man trying to keep the best dogs without any thought of modifying the breed. Even without any change in the proportional numbers of the animals on which our wolf preyed, a cub might be born with an innate tendency to pursue certain kinds of prey.

(Darwin, 1859, p.138)

COMMENT _____

1   In the first instance, a change in environment has affected the wolf's feeding. Those wolves that can most easily catch deer have a potential advantage. If the change lasts for a long time there will be pressure for the wolf population to become more specialized at preying on deer. The last sentence in the extract suggests that environmental changes are not absolutely necessary. Chance may have it that a change occurs in newborn wolves (making them more likely to pursue a deer), and this *can* lead to a species level shift.

2   In time the wolves will change their environment. If they become so adept at killing deer, the latter's population may start to fall. The fall may help other animals to become established or more numerous. In doing so they may well provide new prey for the wolves. The change in wolf characteristics has the potential to produce a change in environment, which can produce a change in wolf characteristics, and so on.

3   This is a more difficult question, but you may have thought about domestic dogs and their sociability. Wolves are social animals, they interact with each other. They hunt in packs, communicate, share cub-rearing duties and so on. This social behaviour may mean that cubs that are not from fast parents may well survive to breed, and may have other roles in the pack than making the kill. Darwin was aware that co-operation within a species group and even between species would also produce evolutionary pressures.

_____

We can summarize Darwin's ideas on evolution as follows:

● Offspring inherit characteristics from their parents. This will never be a perfect copy, there will be small variations. So species can remain largely stable as 'like begets like', but there is also the possibility for change through variation. Species are therefore potentially dynamic.

● A species' environment will also be dynamic, so some of these individual variations may well go on to be positive attributes. If so, they are likely to be reproduced in future generations. This is what is meant by the term 'natural selection'.

● The dynamic characteristics of species and of environments are not independent of one another – they produce change in one another.

Partly on account of the fact that he was writing at a time of free market expansion and numerous wars, Darwin tended to emphasize the brutal, competitive and survivalist aspects of this process. For our purposes here, we need only note that Darwin's work provides a sophisticated account of the interactions between members of a species and their environment that can, but do not necessarily, lead to changes in both the species being and the environment.

SUMMARY

- Species are generally explained with reference to changes that have occurred through time.
- Evolution is the term used to capture this dynamic process.
- Darwin's understanding of evolution took into account the interactions between species members and their environments.

2.2 Evolution and genes

Darwin collected masses of evidence from the field and from talking to domestic animal breeders in order to develop his ideas on evolution through selection. He did not, however, have much evidence for the mechanisms of inheritance and variation. Evidence for this part of the puzzle only really started to be produced in the twentieth century (although important work was done in the 1860s, this remained undiscovered for several decades). Inheritance of parental and species character came to be explained with reference to genes. Genes are giant molecules of DNA (deoxyribonucleic acid) which are organized in such a way that they can carry the necessary information to allow a more or less similar individual to its carrier to be reproduced. (Variation will occur when sexual reproduction involves the combination of genes from two parents, and when the gene copy inevitably becomes garbled in the copying process.) We will have more to say on genes in a moment. For now it is worth noting that as the form and role of genes increasingly became the focus of excitement and investigation, so attention turned away from the interactions between a species and its environment, and more towards the internal properties of genes. In short, species being and evolution started to be thought of as a matter of genetic inheritance and variation. Species-environment interrelationships became a less popular form of explanation.

One group who are particularly prone to use genetic explanations are often known as neo-Darwinists. They take the inheritance and variation parts of Darwin's work to suggest that the main unit of interest when we are trying to explain species' characteristics is genetic material. Their argument leads them to look at genetic DNA as the blueprint of an organism. This blueprint contains the instructions for the development of the organism. If the right conditions are met for the survival of the organism, then this blueprint will work to produce the organism 'according to plan'.

It is worth noting that, in this version of evolution, the environment is very much in the background. The argument is that the genetically-determined characteristics of an organism equip it to survive within a set of conditions (their environment) over which they have little control or influence. If these conditions are not met then they will die out and somebody or something else will take their place. In this, there is no real sense in which the organism and the environment interact in the ways that Darwin was prone to suggest (without having the language of genes). Even though these biologists and geneticists call themselves neo-Darwinists, unlike Darwin they tend to see a clear distinction between genes and their environments.

An alternative understanding of evolution would refuse to focus too heavily on genes and genes alone. Indeed, social scientists are more prone to look for interrelations than to argue that a specific object (like the chemical structure of a large molecule) can explain complex forms and changes. Meanwhile, there is an alternative biology, which also draws on ideas from feminist critiques of science and social science more generally. This biology sees genes as a necessary but not sufficient basis for understanding a species. Mae-Wan Ho, a critic of the neo-Darwinist tendency to see everything as a result of genes, puts it like this:

> When we look at organisms as they are: living, breathing, acting, responding, learning, feeling, developing, and in tune with every aspect of their internal and external environments, it is clear that the fit between organism and environment must arise through reciprocal feedback and adjustments on time scales that range from split seconds to hours, years and even generations. In other words, organisms adapt to the environment and adapt the environment to themselves through continuous processes.
>
> (Ho, 1988, p.122)

We have identified two ways of thinking about genes and evolution. One highlights the *properties* of genes, their shape and their chemistry. In this version, everything you need to understand species' identity is contained within the genetic blueprint. The other view highlights the *interactions* between genes, the organism, other members of a group, and the environment of the species more generally. We can now look at some of the evidence that has been used to justify the former approach, and see how the latter, interactive approach, has been used to criticize a narrow focus on genetic inheritance.

2.2.1 Looking at the evidence for genetic explanations of evolution

If we were to try to understand *Homo sapiens* (the scientific name for the current form of human beings) solely by looking inwards to the chemical structure of our genes and DNA, then we would be faced with the following problem. In terms of their DNA, contemporary humans differ from early humans and chimpanzees by something in the order of 1 per cent. Now, 1 per cent of a massive amount of biological information is still a significant quantity, but this proportion does raise questions about the extent to which species' differences can be predicted solely on the basis of genetic differences. Rather than focus on this 1 per cent of genetic difference alone, the version of evolution that we have called interactive would focus our attention outwards as well as inwards. We would not try to capture the essence of a species or of an individual by looking at the chemical structure of its DNA. Instead, we would look for the interactions between a species or individual and its internal and external nature in order to understand more of its characteristics. We can illustrate these different approaches by focusing on their respective explanations for sexual differences in human beings.

Differences between the sexes are common in many species. As with almost any observed difference between or within species, neo-Darwinists tend to argue in the following way:

1   Describe differences (this depends upon recognizing these in the first place and then on labelling them as important). *Example:* men and women are often described as having different priorities when it comes to choosing partners.

2   Look for the genetic explanation for these differences. *Example:* men and women differ with respect to one chromosome which will contain genes that code for particular characteristics of form and behaviour.

3   Finally, argue that these genetic differences must have been produced through an evolutionary process driven by natural selection.

Here is an example of this kind of argument.

One lengthy research project was carried out by David Buss and his colleagues (1998). Buss starts by mentioning Darwin's theory of sexual selection as being due to animals selecting appropriate mates and competition between males. Following this, Buss suggests that there are possible differences between men's and women's strategies for selecting a mate. He sent questionnaires to over 10,000 people living in 37 different countries. On the basis of the replies, Buss compared men's and women's preferences for long-term mating and short-term mating. Buss reported that men select health and youth as good indicators of reproductive capability. Women's answers showed preferences for men who had the financial resources to care for their mates and children (see Box 1.1).

BOX 1.1   Interpreting bar charts

Figures like Figure 1.2 and Figure 1.3 overleaf are called *bar charts*. Bar charts are particularly convenient for showing a lot of complex data.

Let us first consider Figure 1.2, which shows men's and women's prefence ratings for a mate who is 'a good financial prospect'. The bars in this chart show the number of people who rate the selection of a mate who is a good financial prospect as unimportant or indispensable. If you look at the left-hand column, you will see that the ratings run from unimportant (0) to indispensable (3) at the top. So the higher bars represent ratings which indicate that financial prospects are an indispensable criterion for selecting a mate. The black bars represent women's ratings and the shaded bars represent men's ratings.

With all this information, we can now discuss the interpretation of the data from the Buss survey. The higher bars for women in Figure 1.2 indicate that a greater proportion of women than men reported a preference for a wealthy mate.

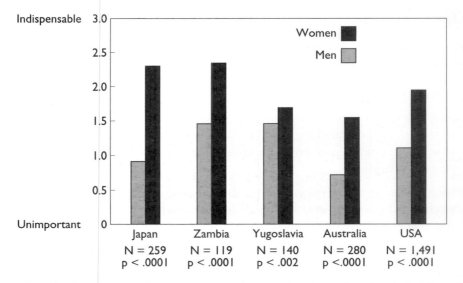

FIGURE 1.2 A sample from Buss *et al.*'s findings showing ratings for desirability of 'good financial prospect' in a long-term mate or marriage partner. (Under each country is the sample size, followed by the statistical significance of the sex difference in value placed on the characteristic. The lower the figure, the more statistical weight can be given to differences between sexes.)

Source: Crawford and Krebs, 1998, Figure 13.3, p.421

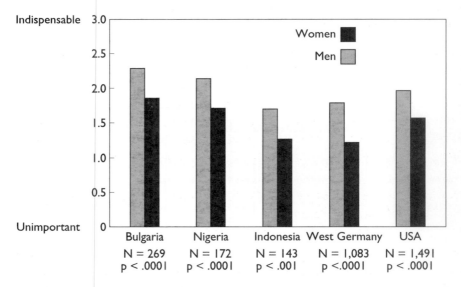

FIGURE 1.3 A sample from Buss *et al.*'s findings showing ratings for desirability of 'physical attractiveness' in a long-term mate or marriage partner. (Under each country is the sample size, followed by the statistical significance of the sex difference in value placed on the characteristic. The lower the figure, the more statistical weight can be given to differences between sexes.)

Source: Crawford and Krebs, 1998, Figure 13.5, p.423

ACTIVITY 1.2

Now look at the black and shaded bars in Figure 1.3. Do more men or women show a preference for a physically attractive mate?

COMMENT _____

The fact that the shaded bars representing men are higher than the black bars for women demonstrates that more men than women rate physical attractiveness as important in selection of a mate. This fits in with the Buss theory that men are looking for physical attractiveness and women for financial security. However, you should note that there are some men looking for financial viability in a mate and some women who are interested in physical attractiveness.

Even if we can believe this data – there are always suspicions that people answer questions in ways that they think they should rather than as a reflection of what they actually do – then to what extent do you think that such differences can be accounted for by genetic differences? Neo-Darwinists argue that women are genetically programmed to behave in this way in order to obtain protection during gestation, birth and looking after children. They are therefore more likely to look for a partner to care for them on a long-term basis. Men, meanwhile, have evolved to be competitive and will therefore be programmed to find as many mates as possible in order to increase the chances of having viable offspring. They will choose on the basis of visual indicators of fertility.

This kind of neo-Darwinist socio-biology is extremely controversial and most social scientists distance themselves from this sort of work. They do so because they think that it makes some gross simplifications of the social world, neglecting to say anything about differences in power and the production of norms and values. Likewise, some biologists also criticize such an approach because it works with an impoverished sense of the interactions between genes and their cellular, organism and more general environments.

What other 'environmental' or 'social' issues do you think might be used to explain the differences that Buss describes?

One answer to this question comes from Angier (1999), a biologist and also a feminist, who provides a different interpretation of Buss's evidence. Angier explains the mating preferences of modern females shown in the Buss surveys as being due to women having less earning power in masculine societies and therefore having an economic incentive to select financially successful men as mates. Meanwhile, social values of companionship along with norms and expectations all contribute to the ways in which people 'select' partners. Attractiveness is also something that is partly learned and reproduced in the media. Selecting partners is therefore a social and natural matter.

In sum, differences and similarities between and within species are sometimes explained by investigating the properties of genes and linking these to Darwinian arguments over natural selection. However, the tendency is to forget that Darwin regarded evolution as an interactive process. We can counter simplistic explanations of species being by accepting that it is the complex of interactions between individuals, their species' characteristics and their social and natural environments that matters.

To return to the differences between *Homo sapiens* and our nearest neighbours, chimpanzees, to what extent do you think that these differences are genetically determined? Our answer would be that, even though the DNA of humans and chimpanzees differs by 1 per cent, there can be little doubt that genes are important. But our differences are also a product of our social relations, cultural processes, the kinds of environments we are born into, the environments we live in, our bodies and so on. These too are passed on from generation to generation but may be inherited through languages, norms, values and so on. This is not to deny that there are real differences between and within species, but it is to say that difference is produced through more complex and interactive processes than we are sometimes led to believe by the neo-Darwinists. The implication is that, if we are not simply a product of our genes but are instead a product of our interrelations (with each other, with outer and inner natures), then the quality of our social and natural environments becomes a vital issue.

We will now extend these arguments by looking at genetic inheritance and intelligence in Section 3 and 4. Our question becomes, were you born intelligent or are you learning how to become intelligent?

SUMMARY

- Since Darwin, evolutionary arguments have tended to focus upon inner nature in order to explain species' differences.

- Genes have become celebrated as the primary units of inheritance and evolution.

- Neo-Darwinists differ from Darwin in that they tend to play down the importance of organism-environment interactions in producing difference and change.

- Social scientists and some biologists argue that social and natural interactions are as important as, if not more important than, chemical and biological properties of genes.

- One implication of this interactive approach to evolution is that the quality of our social and natural environment becomes a crucial matter for the human species.

3   ARE PEOPLE DIFFERENT?

3.1   Inheritance of genes

In the previous section, the emphasis was on the evolution of the whole human species. We are now moving on to the issue of explaining why individual humans are so different from one another. Is the main reason for human diversity that individuals inherit different genes from their parents, or can differences be accounted for by the different environments in which children grow up? What is the relationship between the natural and the social in producing human differences?

Genes are inherited from both parents. The fertilized egg cell includes half the genes from the mother and half the genes from the father. Since all brothers and sisters inherit genes from the same parents there will be family resemblances. But the particular mix of genes will be different for each child.

Can you think of any people who have the same genetic inheritance?

The obvious answer is identical twins. Cloning would also replicate the same genetic structure, although unlike identical twins the inheritance would be from one rather than two individuals.

As we have seen, questions are often asked about whether characteristics like intelligence, creativity, aggressive behaviour, a predisposition to depression or diseases like cancer can be explained by the genes each individual inherits. Does a particular mix of genes make individuals more likely to be intelligent, depressed or aggressive? What causes some people to be much more aggressive than others?

Francis Galton, who published *Hereditary Genius: An Enquiry into Its Laws and Consequences* in 1869, investigated families like the Bach family who were good at music for three generations. The Darwin and Huxley families intermarried, producing not only Charles Darwin and Galton himself, who was a cousin of Charles Darwin, but many other eminent scientists.

Galton claimed that this demonstrated that abilities are inherited from one generation to the next. Can you think of an alternative reason why these abilities might run in families?

It could be that the children of each generation are helped by living in an environment in which music or science are normal activities and expected of the child. This makes it impossible to separate out whether qualities that run through families are inherited or whether they are due to living in a family environment which encourages certain talents.

Galton was also the first person to publish a type of intelligence test based on the speed with which people could react to and distinguish signals. Such tests, as we shall now see, have been used extensively to study inheritance. For reasons that will become clear, a good deal of this work has been undertaken with twins.

3.2 Studies of twins

In order to test the inheritance of abilities more precisely, studies have used twins. The usual comparison is between **identical twins** and **non-identical twins**. Identical twins come from a single fertilized egg and so initially receive exactly the same genetic inheritance from each parent.

Identical twins
Two human individuals produced by a single fertilized egg.

Non-identical twins
Two humans produced by two separate eggs fertilized at the same time.

In twin studies, non-identical twins of the same sex are usually compared with identical twins. Why do you think this is?

Identical twins are always the same sex, either both boys or both girls. Non-identical twins are also selected from the same sex to ensure that both sets of twins are strictly comparable and are not subject to gender-differentiated treatment.

Who would you expect to show more similarity, identical twins or non-identical twins?

Because identical twins share an identical genetic inheritance it would be expected that they would be more similar; for example, on intelligence scores and other qualities. Non-identical twins, who come from different egg cells, share fewer genes and would be expected to show fewer similarities.

IQ
Intelligence quotient is an age-related measure of intelligence.

IQ test
Any test which claims to measure intelligence, usually involving a standardized, graded set of tasks.

Much of the research looking at identical and non-identical twins has the aim of discovering whether differences in intelligence are the result of differences in genetic inheritance. The first question is to consider how it is possible to measure intelligence. The most usual measure is an **IQ** test. Many of us will have taken an **IQ test** at some stage of our lives. Some examples are shown in Box 1.2.

BOX 1.2   Examples from intelligence (IQ) tests

NUMBER CODE

In this test you will be asked to use a number code based on twenty symbols instead of the ten digits to which we are accustomed. There is a symbol for each of the numbers from 0 to 19, as shown below. Notice that a bar means 5 and that a dot means 1. For example, the number 9 is represented by a symbol consisting of a bar and four dots. Zero is represented by a U-shaped symbol as shown.

0	1	2	3	4	5	6	7	8	9
U	.	..	...	....	—	.̲	.̲.̲	.̲.̲.̲	.̲.̲.̲.̲

10	11	12	13	14	15	16	17	18	19

For numbers larger than nineteen, the symbols are combined, one above the other. This is shown in Example 2 below. When there are two symbols, one above the other, the upper one is to be multiplied by 20 and the bottom symbol is to be multiplied by 1. The answer is the sum. Study Example 2.

For numbers larger than 399, three symbols are used, one above the other. The uppermost symbol is multiplied by 400, the next by 20, and the bottom symbol by 1. The answer is the sum. Study Example 3.

Example 1	Example 2	Example 3
.. × 1 = 7	. × 20 = 120	... × 400 = 1200
	.. × 1 = 7	... × 20 = 160
	1̲2̲7̲	.. × 1 = 12
		1372

Now solve the six practice problems below. The first two have already been solved for you.

	Space for figuring	Answer		Space for figuring	Answer
...	× 1 = 13	13	...		
			....		
..	× 20 = 140				
U	× 1 = 0	140	....		
..			U		
....			.		

FIGURE 1.4   Sample test item: numerical ability

Source: Eysenck. 1953. pp.47–8

VERBAL RELATIONS

Read the following row of words:

1-foot: 2-shoe 3-hand: 4-thumb 5-head 6-glove 7-finger
8-clasp   6

The first two words, *foot* and *shoe*, are united by a certain relation, the shoe is worn on the foot. The next word is *hand*. Which of the five words following can be combined with *hand* in the way given by the *foot-shoe* relation? The answer is *glove* because the glove is worn on the hand. Therefore a 6 is written in the blank at the right.

In the following two exercises find the word at the right which is related to the third word in the same way that the second word is related to the first. Write the corresponding numbers in the blanks at the right.

1-fish: 2-water 3-bird: 4-blue 5-robin 6-ocean
7-sky   8-high   _____

1-mayor: 2-city 3-captain: 4-ship 5-private
6-general 7-store 8-lieutenant   _____

FIGURE 1.5   Sample test item: verbal relations
Source: Eysenck, 1953, p.43

WORD-MAKING

Make as many different words as you can, using only the letters in the word G-E-N-E-R-A-T-I-O-N-S. You may use long or short words and may include the names of persons, places, or foreign words. In any one word do not use a letter more times than it appears in G-E-N-E-R-A-T-I-O-N-S.

Sample words have been written in the first few lines. Continue writing as many words as you can using only the letters given.

G-E-N-E-R-A-T-I-O-N-S

1. *art*
2. *era*
3. *snore*
4. _____
5. _____

FIGURE 1.6   Sample test item: word-making
Source: Eysenck, 1953, p.46

ACTIVITY 1.3

How many of these tests do you think measure intelligence? For which tests is cultural knowledge important for achieving high scores?

COMMENT _____

Most of the tests measure problem-solving skills in the abstract rather than in the world of social relations and experience. There are certainly no tests in Box 1.2 of what has been called *social intelligence* – the ability to understand other people's intentions and to react appropriately, to make choices and to implement them taking into account social and moral situations. The skills required for successful performance in IQ tests, including speed of completion, can be practised, so that in this sense it would be possible to learn some of these skills.

Those who advocate their use consider that numerical IQ tests (like the item shown in Figure 1.4) and spatial tests are culture free. This is because the abilities to use numbers and to recognize shapes are supposed to be universal, regardless of the culture in which you grow up. This may itself be an unjustified assumption. These abilities may be potentially available to everyone, but educational experience will be crucial in developing these skills.

These considerations apply even more to verbal tests (see Figure 1.5), which are totally dependent on 'Western' knowledge which is only available in certain cultures. For example, these tests may be completely mysterious to children in other countries who may never have seen a robin or an ocean. Tests like word-making (Figure 1.6) depend on having a large vocabulary in order to achieve a high IQ score. Verbal tests put children who have not had the chance to acquire this kind of knowledge at a distinct disadvantage.

It is well known that some people perform particularly well on logical IQ tests. Others, even within the same culture and with the same educational experience, are better at open-ended tests. One example of an open-ended task would be the word-making test of generating words from a longer word (e.g. 'generations', as in Figure 1.6). This depends on thinking up as many words as you can. Liam Hudson (1966), in his study of schoolboys, called the boys who were good at solving logical problems *convergers* because they converge on one correct answer. In addition to word-generating tests, Hudson introduced other open-ended tests. One asked, 'How many uses can you think of for a brick?' Boys were scored not only on the number of uses they could think of but also on how unusual and imaginative their answers were. Those who were good at generating words and uses of bricks were called *divergers* because they had to diverge, to go off on a tangent of lateral thinking, in order to come up with novel ideas.

If the first question was to consider how intelligence could be measured, the next step (despite the reservations above) was to give twins IQ tests. The aim was to test whether the IQ scores of identical twins were more similar than the IQ scores of non-identical twins. If identical twins have more similar IQ scores, this would be interpreted as favouring heredity, the similarity in scores being attributed to the identical genetic inheritance of identical twins.

You may be wondering how researchers measured the similarities between identical twins as compared with non-identical twins. The main technique used is to calculate correlations. Box 1.3 gives a simple account of how to interpret correlations. The point is that numbers are calculated to indicate similarity.

Correlation

A relationship between two (or more) sets of data so that changes in one set are accompanied by systematic increases or decreases in the other.

BOX 1.3   Correlations

The usual method of comparing whether twins' scores are similar is to calculate a **correlation** between their scores. Correlations measure the degree to which two sets of measures are similar. A 'perfect' correlation of 1.0 means that the scores are completely related. A correlation of 0 shows that the scores are in no way alike.

Look at the IQ scores for seven pairs of identical twins in Table 1.1.

TABLE 1.1 Intelligence (IQ) scores for identical twins

	Twin 1	Twin 2
Twin pair 1	10	8
Twin pair 2	5	4
Twin pair 3	9	11
Twin pair 4	6	6
Twin pair 5	8	7
Twin pair 6	2	3
Twin pair 7	7	9

From these scores it may appear that the IQ scores are not at all the same for the different pairs of twins. But if you look more closely you will see that each pair of twins shares the same levels of scores. For instance, pair 1, pair 3 and pair 5 share high scores. Pair 6 both have low scores. The calculated correlation for these seven pairs of scores is 0.8. This is a high correlation because 0.8 is nearly 1.0 which would show that the scores are perfectly related. Now let us look at Table 1.2 which shows IQ scores for seven pairs of non-identical twins.

TABLE I.2   Intelligence (IQ) scores for non-identical twins

	Twin I	Twin 2
Twin pair I	10	8
Twin pair 2	4	5
Twin pair 3	6	I
Twin pair 4	2	4
Twin pair 5	7	3
Twin pair 6	I	6
Twin pair 7	9	9

This time you can see that not all the twin pairs have the same levels of scores. Pair I both have high scores and pair 2 both have medium scores. But in the case of the pair 3 twins, the first twin has a score of 6 and the other twin only has a score of I.

The calculated correlation for these seven pairs of scores is 0.25. This is a much lower correlation than the 0.8 for the identical twins. This would be interpreted as showing that the IQ scores for identical twins are more similar (high correlation of 0.8) than the IQs scores for non-identical twins (low correlation of 0.25).

Many studies have compared the IQ scores of identical and non-identical twins. But one problem is that when twins are brought up together they share the same culture and environment. It may be that a common environment and being brought up by the same parents are the real reasons for the similar IQ scores. It can also be argued that identical twins are treated more alike, even being dressed the same, which could be a possible explanation for the greater similarity in their IQ scores.

In order to rule out a similar environment as a possible explanation, researchers have tried to find identical twins who have been separated at birth and brought up in different environments by different carers. The argument is that, because each twin will have been reared in a different family environment, any similarities found between them must be due to their identical genetic inheritance rather than to similar social experiences. Early studies up to the 1960s showed relatively high correlations between the IQs of quite large numbers of pairs of separated identical twins, ranging from 0.62 to 0.8. These significantly high correlations have been claimed as indicating a high proportion of genetic inheritance. There is, however, other evidence which favours more environmental or interactive explanations.

3.3 Adoption studies

Children who are adopted early in life share none of their genes with their adoptive parents but 50 per cent of the inheritance supplied by their birth mothers. (We are using 'birth mother' to mean the mother who provides the egg which contributes half of the child's genetic inheritance. This is usually the mother who gives birth to the child. However, there are also 'host mothers' who gestate and give birth to the child formed from the fertilized egg of another woman.) It is reasonable to assume that, if differences are due mainly to environmental factors, then the IQs of adopted children should be more like those of their adoptive parents than those of their birth mothers with whom the children have never lived. Early researchers found that IQs of adopted children were highly correlated with those of their birth mothers, even for children adopted before the age of 6 months. For decades this finding was considered to be the most powerful evidence showing the genetic inheritance of IQ to be high. This is because there seemed to be no possible environmental explanation for such a high correlation between the IQs of children and the IQs of their birth mothers from whom they had been separated in early infancy.

Later adoption studies focused on parents who have raised both adopted children and their own children (birth children) in the same home. Thus, the children are brought up in the same environment by the same parents. Any significant differences between parents and the adopted children, as compared with the birth children, would be attributed to the fact that only the birth children share genes in common with their parents. However, these studies show that there were in fact equal correlations between the IQs of the mothers and those of the birth children and of the adopted children. The studies can be interpreted as showing that nurture by the same parents in the same environment is the important issue. The different genetic inheritance of the birth and adopted children seems to have no effect on the final outcome.

The earlier studies implied that adopted children have IQs which are similar to the IQs of their birth mothers. This would be an argument for the genetic inheritance of IQ. Later studies indicated that, when the comparison is made between the IQs of mothers and those of their birth and adopted children living in the same home, there were no significant differences in the correlations between the IQs of the mothers and those of the birth and adopted children. This implies that any differences in IQ are due to social experience.

3.4 Criticisms of twin studies of intelligence

There are several arguments which have to be taken into account when trying to interpret the results of research into the heritability of intelligence.

1   The first consideration is that, in order to measure whether characteristics are similar or different, researchers have to choose characteristics which can easily be *measured*. This is one reason why so many studies

concerned with intelligence are measured by IQ tests (see Box 1.2). There has been a lot of criticism about using IQ tests to measure intelligence. They only measure one kind of logical intelligence. The questions rely on knowledge of a particular language and culture so they may not be so easy for people without such culturally specific experiences. IQ tests are not culture-free and children can be coached to improve performance on IQ tests. So all that may be demonstrated is that there are similarities in passing IQ tests, not general intelligence itself.

2   Another possible explanation for similarities in intelligence is called *selective placement.* Children are not delivered to their adoptive homes by storks. They are usually sent there by adoption agencies who tried, especially before the Second World War, to place most children in well-off homes. In the modern period, agencies have generally tied to place each child with adoptive parents whose intellectual and educational level roughly matches that of the birth mother. What follows from this is that any similarity between children's IQs and the IQs of their birth mothers may have been due to selective placement in environments similar to the environments of their birth mothers rather than being the result of genetic factors. Selective placement is even more likely to happen with identical twins. Investigations have shown that more than half of the 'separated' twins were brought up by members of the same family – for example, a mother and aunt living in the same locality with the twins even attending the same school. So similarities between identical twins can at least partly be accounted for by being brought up in similar backgrounds.

3   The third point is that it is practically (and, we would argue, logically) impossible to give a percentage of heredity. Suppose every child has an *identical* social background. Any differences in performance would be interpreted as being due to heredity, which would lead to a *high* estimate of the role played by genetic inheritance. Suppose instead that children have wildly *different* experiences of life. Any differences in performance would be interpreted as being due to the different environments. In this case, there would be a *low* estimate of the part played by genetic inheritance. But the findings are never as extreme as this. The range of possible interactions between genetic and environmental factors makes trying to disentangle their relative importance a futile endeavour.

There are obviously differences between people and the way they interact with the world. Genetic inheritance plays a role, particularly in physical qualities like height and colour of hair and eyes. It is much more difficult to tease out the causes of abilities like intelligence, in which heredity and social experience are intertwined. Nevertheless, it is possible that individuals inherit predispositions to intelligence which may either be stimulated or repressed, depending on gender, class, culture, ethnicity and social experiences. Uncertainty and diversity arise from what some people have called the lottery of the genetic mix inherited from parents and grandparents. Of equal importance is the lottery of experience. Both together produce the great diversity found among human beings.

Although researchers carry out their studies carefully, this is an area in which the theoretical approach of researchers will have an effect. Some researchers believe that it is possible to calculate a specific percentage of heredity which determines human nature. Other researchers are more convinced by the criticisms outlined in this section and believe that the way forward is to emphasize the complicated interaction between genetics and social experiences.

SUMMARY

- Individuals inherit a mixture of genes from both parents, which makes them genetically unique (apart from identical twins).
- Research has been carried out on twins and adopted children with the aim of discovering the role of heredity in intelligence.
- Criticisms of these studies are based on the possibility of twins experiencing similar upbringing as a result of selective placements, the uncritical use of IQ tests and other measurement scales, and a tendency to concentrate on genetic rather than social explanations.
- The utility of twin studies can also be criticized on a more fundamental basis in that it is practically (and, in our terms, logically) impossible to divide the world into matters of nature and nurture. The interactions are so complete that we need to think in ways that are not tied to these purified categories.

4 HOW DO CHILDREN DEVELOP?

4.1 Similarity and difference

Having looked at explanations and evidence for human similarities and differences, we now move to look at the way children develop. In particular, we look at the issues which affect how children grow up to be human adults in human society. As we have seen, one issue concerns the relative importance of genetic inheritance and social conditions in child development. When this question is applied to child development, the genetic and biological make-up of a child is often thought of as making up its 'nature'. This is contrasted with 'nurture', a term which is derived from the quality of 'nursing' which the child receives. Nurture is wider than this as it includes the social situation in which a child is brought up and all the ways in which the family and society impinge on the individual child.

This distinction raises the issue of whether all human babies are genetically preprogrammed to behave in certain ways. The alternative is that, from the earliest months, it is the quality of parenting babies receive, either from parents or other carers, which determines their future. The latter approach would emphasize the importance of nurture in a child's development.

Can you think of any evidence that might be relevant to this debate?

At an anectotal level, mothers often comment on what their baby is like, quiet or rumbustious. This is at such a very early stage that it would suggest that babies are born with their own personalities. Parents also comment on when their child first smiles, crawls or talks. These milestones would appear to be preprogrammed stages for which all babies are genetically prepared.

There is, however, also evidence of the effects of nurture, or lack of nurture, on children's development. Starting with John Bowlby's work on maternal deprivation in the 1960s, there is evidence of the devastating effects of being deprived of a carer. Bowlby (1973) observed very young children who had been separated from their mothers, for instance in hospital or in care. He described how at first the children cry and display emotional responses. If the period of separation is extended, the children become apathetic and in general behave as if they did not care. When the mother returns she will be greeted with tantrums and rage rather than affection.

Bowlby's theory is a good example of the crucial role of nurture in child development. His research is also an interesting case study of the way in which research can be taken up for political purposes. Although Bowlby's own research was well conducted, his results have been used as part of a campaign to discourage women with children from working outside the home and keep mothers at home caring for their children. When there is a demand for women in the labour market and a policy of encouraging women to work outside the home, far less is heard about the devastating effects of maternal deprivation and far more about the quality of care by other carers. More positively, Bowlby's work has been influential in promoting more child-friendly policies in hospitals – for example, allowing open visiting and parents to stay overnight with their sick children.

Bowlby's work highlighted the importance of the care which children receive to their own psychological development. Other psychologists have focused more on the internal cognitive processes of child development.

4.2 Piaget's theory of cognitive development

FIGURE 1.7   Jean Piaget

Jean Piaget, a pioneering child psychologist who worked on children's cognitive development, was born in Switzerland in 1896 and lived until 1980. Like Bowlby, Piaget studied young children. Whereas Bowlby was mainly concerned with social and emotional development, Piaget studied the development of intelligence and the ways in which children become aware of their environment and of the intentions of other people.

Piaget's prolific writings have had an extremely wide impact. Educationalists, particularly those concerned with younger children, were quick to use his ideas in developing new teaching methods. 'Discovery learning', 'learning through play' and 'reading readiness' were developed in the 1950s and 1960s with explicit reference to Piaget's work. But his findings, and his interpretations of them, are not accepted without question.

Piaget started his career as a biologist, interested particularly in the processes by which organisms adapt intelligently to their environment during development. His interest in the development of children began in 1920 when he was invited to work in Alfred Binet's laboratory in Paris, helping to translate into French items originally developed by Cyril Burt in England for the very first intelligence test. An intelligence test focuses on items children get right, but Piaget soon became interested in the underlying reasons for children sometimes giving wrong answers to the questions asked. These 'errors' seemed to him to be systematic rather than random, pointing towards some underlying consistencies in the children's developing mental abilities.

Piaget devised various methods for discovering what children really think and how their thinking differs from adult thinking. Piaget believed that the language used by children will reveal misconceptions they have about the world. Some of Piaget's earliest research was to observe young children at a Swiss kindergarten. In Switzerland, in Piaget's time, children stayed in kindergarten until 6–7 years old, only beginning school at the age of 7 plus. Piaget noted that the children often spoke to describe their own actions and took very little notice of other children's speech. Piaget called this **egocentric speech**. Egocentric referred to the fact that young children's impressions of the world are centred around themselves and they find it difficult to see things from another point of view or to imagine how

Egocentric speech
Speech which derives from and serves the individual's own needs. It is focused on the self.

other people might perceive and understand the world. Piaget also used the term **collective monologue** to describe how each child carries on with their own monologue as if talking to others but not to the children they are with (Piaget, 1926).

Collective monologue
Speech which is carried out in the presence of others but which is lacking in any real communication.

BOX 1.4   **Piaget's methods for observing speech**

One method Piaget used was to record all the speech of some of the children in the kindergarten. The following extracts give examples of how Pie, who was 6 years old, interacted with some friends while they were drawing various objects:

Pie (to Ez who is drawing a tram-car with carriages in tow): *But the trams that are hooked on behind don't have any flags.* (No answer.)

(Talking about his tram). *They don't have any carriages hook on ...* (He was addressing no one in particular. No one answers him.)

(To Béa), *'Tsa tram that hasn't got no carriages.* (No answer.)

(To Hei), *This tram hasn't got no carriages, Hei, look, it isn't red, d'you see ...* (No answer.)

(Lev says out loud, 'A funny gentleman' from a certain distance, and without addressing himself to Pie or anyone else). Pie: *A funny gentleman!* (Goes on drawing his tram.)

I'm leaving the tram white.

(Ez who is drawing next to him says, 'I'm doing it yellow'), *No, you mustn't do it all yellow.*

(Piaget, 1926/1962, pp.6–7)

ACTIVITY 1.5

Which aspects of the recorded conversation show evidence of egocentric speech and collective monologue?

COMMENT _____

Pie (probably short for Pierre) continues a collective monologue to describe the train he is drawing and colouring although none of the other children is taking any notice of his comments. Repeating Lev's remark about 'A funny gentleman' is an example of egocentric speech since Pie has no notion who is being referred to.

BOX 1.5   **Piaget's question and answer sessions**

Piaget and his colleagues also used to ask children about natural events in order to reveal their misconceptions about the causes of events:

Cam, aged 6, said of the sun: *'It comes with us to look at us.*

Why does it look at us?

It looks to see if we are good.

Why does the moon move?

It's time to go and work. Then the moon comes.

Why does it move?

Because it's going to work with the men who work.

Do you believe that?

Yes.

That it works?

It looks to see if they work properly.'

Another child, aged 6, said that the *'sun goes with me when I walk'* and it is the wind that makes the sun move because the wind knows where I am going.

(Piaget, 1930)

Piaget interpreted the children's answers as showing that even 6-year-old children believe that the moon and sun revolve around themselves and their own activities, another example of egocentric thinking.

What problems can you see with this method of asking children questions?

One criticism is that when adults ask children what may seem very mysterious questions, the children try to second guess what answers the adult may be expecting. Some of the questions may have been 'leading questions' which make it obvious what the adult was after. The use of leading questions by a lawyer to extract answers from witnesses is quite rightly criticized by the judge.

A second problem is that there is a limit to the kinds of thinking which can be asked about in this way. Adults may use preconceived categories which limit and predetermine children's responses.

4.3   Stages of intellectual development

Based on observations of early child language and what they reveal about children's ways of thinking, Piaget produced a general theory of child development. He believed that all children inevitably progress through various stages of cognitive development. He was interested in charting the gradual development of mental abilities like being able to think about problems, find appropriate solutions, or learn about history and mathematics.

Piaget's theory sets out the stages at which children develop intellectual skills as part of their developing intelligence. The important point is that children *cannot skip a stage*. It is impossible to learn mathematics before a child is able to count. On the other hand, although Piaget gave rough ages for each stage, he recognized that children develop at different rates, especially during the many substages of development. These stages suggest inherent human characteristics and emphasize the natural aspects of cognitive development, although as we have seen Piaget's examples are culturally specific.

Stage 1: Sensori-motor (birth to about 2 years)

Piaget observed in his own three children the development of active responses to objects, grasping for them and gradually bringing them under control. The acquisition of language makes an enormous difference which propels children on to the next stage.

Stage 2: Pre-operational (from about 2–7 years old)

The rather odd phrase 'pre-operational' refers to the child's *lack* of logical operations. By this, Piaget means that children of this age do not understand the real causes of events, as shown by their answers to questions. They also go by appearances and fail to appreciate the underlying logic of numerical operations. They are egocentric and cannot understand another person's point of view.

Stage 3: Operational (about 7–12 years old)

At this stage children begin to understand the underlying logical and numerical operations carried out in relation to *concrete* objects which they can actually see. They begin to understand other people's intentions and other points of view.

Stage 4: Formal operations (12 years upwards)

At this stage logical operations can be applied to understanding *abstract* systems like mathematics, and logic can be used as a tool to think about events which are distanced in time or place.

Most of Piaget's research was aimed at showing how children's intellectual skills during the pre-operational period differ from those of older 'operational' children. Because of the limitations of simply talking to children, Piaget set himself the task of finding methods for demonstrating intelligence in action, using imaginative approaches to work out new ways of demonstrating intelligence.

Naturalistic experiments
Experiments conducted in actual situations, not in a laboratory.

He used what are called **naturalistic experiments** in which children are asked to solve real-life problems. In psychology, these are contrasted with laboratory experiments in which people are required to perform tasks in a strictly uniform environment and every aspect of their behaviour is measured precisely.

One of Piaget's most famous natural experiments concerns the ability of children to realize that elements like water and numbers of objects remain the same, regardless of superficial changes. Piaget called this **conservation** because older children and adults realize that elements and numbers are conserved; that is, they do not change.

Conservation
The recognition that elements like water do not change even if they 'look' different.

The best way to demonstrate the conservation method is to show you some of the situations invented by Piaget. The most famous of these is the water jugs problem. This is shown in Box 1.6.

BOX 1.6   Conservation experiments

Piaget's classic conservation of liquid task was devised to give a standard way of assessing an individual's level of intellectual development. It involves three basic steps:

1   First, the child is shown two identical transparent beakers. A and B, each about two-thirds full of water, as shown in Figure 1.8. These are placed side-by-side in front of the child. The experimenter seeks the child's agreement that the quantity of water in each beaker is the same, if necessary adding or taking away small amounts until the child is satisfied.

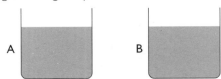

FIGURE 1.8   Initial display in the conservation of water task

2   As shown in Figure 1.9, the water from one beaker, A, is then poured into another beaker, A2, which is either taller and narrower than the first one, or shorter and wider.

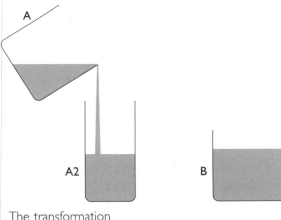

FIGURE 1.9   The transformation

3   This beaker is placed alongside beaker B as shown in Figure 1.10. The child
is than asked whether there is now more water in the new beaker, A2,
than in the other beaker, B, or less, or the same amount.

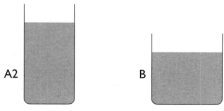

FIGURE 1.10   The transformed display

Typically, up to the age of about 6 or 7 years, children will assert, when asked,
that the amount of liquid has changed, and is now more (or less, depending on
the arrangement and their perception of it). If a child is then asked why this is so,
he or she will tend to say something like 'because it's taller', or because it's
thinner'. Children's answers seem to indicate that their judgement of quantity is
centred on the perceptual change brought about by the transformation.

ACTIVITY 1.6

In Piaget's conservation of number task, the initial, untransformed display consists of
two rows of counters – one row of white counters and one row of black counters –
with an equal number of counters in each row. The two rows are placed side-by-side
in front of the child as shown in Figure 1.11.

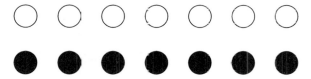

FIGURE 1.11   Initial display of counters in the conservation of numbers task

The row of black counters is then spread out, or placed closer together, so that the
two rows are then of unequal length, but still each having the same number of
counters, as shown in Figure 1.12.

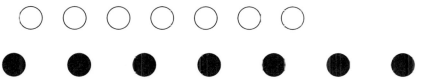

FIGURE 1.12   Transformed display of counters in the conservation of numbers task

Children are then asked whether one line of counters has more than the other, or
the same, or less. When they have answered, they are asked to give reasons for their
reply.

Look at the counters laid out in rows in Figure 1.12.

1 What do you think a pre-operational child aged 4–7 would say if asked how many counters there are in the second row? What reasons might he or she give?

2 What would be the response of an older (operational) child or an adult?

3 What implications would this have for the ability to count and eventually to understand mathematics?

C O M M E N T

1 Pre-operational children tend to say that there are more black counters in the second row (because they cover a greater distance).

2 Older children and adults appreciate that the number of counters is always the same, regardless of how they are laid out.

3 Pre-operational children are unlikely to be able to deal with 'sums' until they master conservation of number, regardless of what the counters look like.

Concrete operations
These involve a child being able to understand operations carried out on physical objects, contrasted with the later stages of formal operations which involve abstract thought.

These examples are called **concrete operations** because they refer to concrete objects like water jugs and counters which can be seen. This is what Piaget means when he says that children have to go through the operational stage of understanding concrete concepts in real life before they can go on to manipulate abstract concepts, in Stage 4, which involve formal operations.

4.4 Later studies of children's intelligence

Most of the research on children's intellectual development has been undertaken to extend or offer criticisms to Piaget's theory. Like Darwin, Piaget has set the scene for future research.

One line of criticism has been that the children in Piaget's studies were presented with what might seem rather odd situations followed by questions about whether the amount of water or counters had increased or decreased. Children always try to make sense of what they see.

Later experiments were carried out to give children a more convincing reason for expressing a view about the conservation of number. For example, Paul Light and his colleagues (Light *et al.*, 1979) asked children to estimate the amount of pasta shells in a jar. When a real reason is given for transferring the contents from one jar to another, more children turn out to be conservers (see Box 1.7).

| BOX I.7 | **The pasta shells experiment** |

In this study, eighty 6-year-olds were tested in pairs. For half of them, the task was a standard Piagetian conservation task. Two identical beakers were filled to the same level with dried pasta shells. When the children agreed that there was the same amount in each beaker the contents of one beaker were poured into a wider beaker. Only 5 per cent of the children said that the quantities were the same: 95 per cent, in other words, appeared to be 'non-conservers'.

For the other half of the children the procedure was different. They were told at the outset that they were going to use the pasta shells in a competitive game. But, after they had agreed that the two identical beakers contained the same amount, the experimenter 'noticed' that one of the beakers was dangerously chipped around the rim. He looked around and found the alternative (larger) beaker and poured the contents in, asking the children before they started their game whether they had the same amount of shells each. This time, 70 per cent of them judged that the quantities were equal: only 30 per cent appeared to be 'non-conservers'.

It may be that the 'game' element was important. When the children were thinking in terms of sharing out the pasta for a game, their attention was focused on 'fair shares'. The chipped beaker gave a sensible, practical reason for transferring one lot of pasta to a different container. Under these conditions, far more children appeared to understand that the number of shells was unaffected by the perceptual change and were thus apparently 'conservers'.

Margaret Donaldson, in her well-known book *Children's Minds* (1978), was one of the first people to report that, in more familiar situations, children could imagine other viewpoints. This is shown in Box 1.8.

| BOX I.8 | **The policeman experiment** |

In this study reported in Donaldson's book, children between 3 years and 5 years of age were tested individually using an apparatus consisting of two walls which intersected to form a cross, as shown in Figure 1.13. In the first stage the child was asked to judge whether a policeman doll could see a 'boy' doll from various positions. Then the child was asked to hide the doll so the policeman could not see him, with the policeman at a given position. Then a second policeman was introduced, as illustrated in Figure 1.13, and the child was asked to hide the doll from both policemen. This required the child to consider and co-ordinate two points of view. Look at Figure 1.13 and work out where the doll should be placed (in this case, the only effective hiding place is at C). This was repeated three times so that each time a different section was left as the only hiding place. The results were clear: 90 per cent of the responses given by the children were correct. This was well below the age when Piaget thought children capable of seeing another's (non-egocentric) point of view. One important factor may have been that the children were asked to *act* in hiding the boy from the policemen rather than simply answering questions.

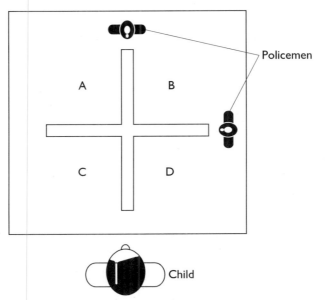

FIGURE 1.13   Plan of the experimental layout in the policeman experiment
Source: Donaldson, 1978

In view of later research, Piaget has been criticized for not allowing a sufficient role for social experience, although he emphasized the socialization of actions through speech and later through games and rules. Even in his earliest work on language, he gave examples of how children gradually learn to co-operate in exchanging ideas. As he also points out, very young children go through the motions when playing games. It is only when children are 7 or 8 years old that they realize that games have rules and that someone can win or lose. However, although Piaget agreed that experience was necessary, he showed little interest in the practicalities of interacting with other people, parents, teachers and other children. Somehow there is a feeling of inevitability about Piaget's universal stages of child development from earliest childhood to adolescence.

Stages of smiling, talking and reaching out to objects are virtually universal. It has been suggested that these gestures may have naturally evolved to engage carers during the long childhood of the infant. As Piaget suggests, there is no way that a 2 to 3-year-old who can talk will be able to take other people's views into account, answer questions about the moon or pay attention to the amount of water in jugs. However, even at this early stage, nurture can have an enormous effect. If no-one talks to a child or takes much notice of it, development will be slow if it takes place at all. There are a few tragic cases in which wild children growing up with animals, or children found shut up in attics, have not learned human language or how to socialize with other people. These are, of course, extreme examples, but there are many degrees of poor to excellent nurturing experiences.

Jerome Bruner challenged the fixity of Piaget's developmental stages and asserted the much greater influence of social interventions in facilitating the child's cognitive development. Bruner has always stressed the importance of interactions between mother and infant for developing social relationships. In his book *Child's Talk* (1983), Bruner stressed the importance of children learning to become agents for their own behaviour as a result of long periods of talk between baby and mother. Bruner gives some useful examples of how mothers and children gradually negotiate a mapping of words on to concepts in the environment. At earlier stages, a mother might accept a child's use of 'nice' to describe, for example, friendly animals, leaving it until the child is ready to make more subtle ethical distinctions.

Bruner refers to mothers because he studied pairs of mothers and children Others have studied 'motherese', the special language mothers use to communicate with children. These findings would apply to anyone who acts as the primary carer of the child. Bruner, too, was writing before so many children have the experience of family break-ups. Nevertheless, Bruner's observations of mother–child speech, which stress the interaction between mother and child and the agency which the child too can exercise, has been developed extensively and applied to parenting and education. Bruner's work has suggested that children's learning can be facilitated by appropriate teaching methods. We do not have to wait until a child has reached the cognitive stage of being 'ready to read'; interesting, engaging material and interaction can pre-empt 'stages' of development.

There are some uniformities about the early stages of child development – when children are ready for schooling, or for leaving the home – although what is thought to be appropriate may vary across different societies. There are so many cultural and material circumstances which can affect how these stages are implemented. Expectations can vary from family to family and be affected by class, gender, divorce and income, even within one community. There are obviously enormous differences worldwide – the social and the natural interconnect in complex ways.

SUMMARY

- Piaget's theory postulates four stages of child development from birth to adolescence. These have been interpreted as the result of universal evolution of children's progress to become intelligent human beings.

- Piaget's theory is concerned with the development of the intellectual mind (cognitive development). He carried out observations and experiments to demonstrate what children are capable of.

- These observations involved adult, culturally specific interpretation of children's speech and actions.

- Later psychologists like Donaldson and Bruner have shown that children react better to more familiar situations, and that infant–parent interactions and other social aspects are crucial for development, emphasizing more explicitly the interrelationship between the natural and the social.

- Cognitive development, as illustrated by children's language and behaviour, involves connections between internal cognitive processes and social, cultural circumstances, including adult carers and teachers.

5 CONCLUSION

This chapter has focused upon the natural and the social interactions that produce both human similarity and difference. Throughout the chapter we have argued that social scientists need to resist explanations of human behaviour and character that refer solely to genetic inheritance. Rather, we should focus upon the interactions between genes, people and their social and natural environments in order to understand more of what it means to be human. Inner nature in the form of genes is therefore not so much a rigid structure that determines what we do. Instead, our biological inheritance can be viewed as a set of possible constraints, but *at the same time* it is a resource that can enable us to live our lives in multifaceted and varied ways. In other words, it is a *structure* that also allows for the possibility of agency.

Our focus on intelligence in this chapter has allowed us to consider the mechanisms through which the natural and biological interconnects with the social. Differences in learning abilities and intelligence are clearly prefigured by biological inheritance, but this is in no way thought to determine a person's development. When we look more closely, it even becomes impossible to disentangle this inheritance from what are more often called social matters. Put crudely, genes need the right environment to do their work. A child's development will depend upon a range of issues – from prenatal care, to general nurturing, to a whole range of environmental and social interactions.

This chapter has also focused on how we investigate these social and natural interrelationships. We have looked closely at social science experimentation and observation, and we have considered the kinds of evidence that they produce. We have also criticized some methods, such as intelligence testing by means of IQ tests, for being too artificial or for not taking into account their own assumptions.

To return to the points made in the introduction to the chapter, we can see how social science approaches can prove useful at a time when there is increasing uncertainty over what makes us human. Issues like human cloning and gene therapy are not easy matters upon which to offer clear answers, but an enriched understanding of the social life as well as the natural life of our genes may help us make more informed decisions in the future. This commitment to the importance of natural and social interrelationships is taken up in the three remaining chapters in this book.

REFERENCES

Angier, N. (1999) *Women: An Intimate Geography*, London, Virago Press.

Bowlby, J. (1973) *Attachment and Loss*, London, The Hogarth Press.

Bruner, J. (1983) *Child's Talk*, Oxford, Oxford University Press.

Buss, D.M. (1998) 'The psychology of human mate selection: exploring the complexity of the strategic repertoire' in Crawford, C. and Krebs, D.L. (eds).

Crawford, C. and Krebs, D.L. (eds) (1998) *Handbook of Evolutionary Psychology: Ideas, Issues and Applications*, London, Lawrence Erlbaum Associates.

Darwin, C. (1859) *The Origin of Species by Means of Natural Selection*, London, John Murray.

Donaldson, M. (1978) *Children's Minds*, London, Fontana/Collins.

Eysenck, H. (1953) *Uses and Abuses of Psychology*, Harmondsworth, Penguin.

Flavel, J.H. (1963) *The Developmental Psychology of Jean Piaget*, New York, D. Van Nostrand.

Galton, F. (1869) *Hereditary Genius: An Enquiry into Its Laws and Consequences*, 2nd edn (reprinted 1978), London, Julian Friedmann.

Gove, J. and Watt, S. (2000) 'Identity and gender' in Woodward, K. (ed.).

Ho, M.-W. (1988) 'On not holding nature still: evolution by process, not by consequence' in Ho, M.-W. and Fox, S. (eds) *Evolutionary Processes and Metaphors*, Chichester, Wiley.

Hudson, L. (1966) *Contrary Imaginations: A Psychological Study of the English Schoolboy*, London, Methuen.

Lewontin, R. (1993) *The Doctrine of DNA: Biology as Ideology*, Harmondsworth, Penguin.

Light, P., Buckingham, N. and Robbins, N. (1979) 'The conservation task as an interactional setting', *British Journal of Educational Psychology*, vol.49, part 3, pp.304–10.

Mooney, G., Kelly, B., Goldblatt, D. and Hughes, G. (2000) DD100 *Introductory Chapter. Tales of Fear and Fascination: The Crime Problem in the Contemporary UK*, Milton Keynes, The Open University.

Piaget, J. (1926/1962) *Language and Thought of the Child* (3rd edn), London, Routledge and Kegan Paul.

Piaget, J. (1930) *The Child's Conception of Physical Causality*, London, Routledge and Kegan Paul.

Rose, H. (1998) 'Moving on from both state and consumer eugenics?' in Braun, B. and Castree, N. (eds) *Remaking Reality: Nature at the Millennium*, Routledge, London.

Woodward, K. (ed.) (2000) *Questioning Identity: Gender, Class, Nation*, London, Routledge/The Open University.

FURTHER READING

An excellent summary of the shortcomings of neo-Darwinist socio-biology is provided by the biologist Richard Lewontin in *The Doctrine of DNA: Biology as Ideology.* (Harmondsworth, Penguin, 1993). Lewontin explores the history of our genetic fixation and investigates IQ and twin evidence in some detail.

Jean Piaget was an extremely prolific writer and his books give a vivid account of the development of his theories about the development of intelligence. Three of the most accessible are: *Language and Thought of the Child* (London, Routledge and Kegan Paul, 1926); *The Child's Conception of Physical Causality* (London, Routledge and Kegan Paul, 1930); and *The Moral Judgement of the Child* (London, Routledge and Kegan Paul, 1932). Still one of the best handbooks describing Piaget's theories and research is *The Developmental Psychology of Jean Piaget*, by J.H. Flavel (New York, D. Van Nostrand, 1963).

One of the books which threw doubt on purely intellectual development was Margaret Donaldson's small but influential book *Children's Minds* (London, Fontana/Collins, 1978). This describes some of the first experiments to show that it makes a difference if a cognitive task is formulated in a way that makes sense to the child.

Whose health is it anyway?

Brenda Smith and David Goldblatt

Contents

1	**Introduction**	**44**
2	**'Natural' explanations: medical conceptions of health and illness**	**48**
	2.1 The relation between the body and the mind: notions of health and illness	48
	2.2 Effective understanding	51
3	**Social explanations: the impact of social class**	**53**
4	**Complex interactions: the complementary health movement**	**57**
	4.1 The body and the mind: holistic approaches	59
	4.2 Effective understanding	61
5	**The New Public Health: the decline of illness and the rise of health**	**62**
	5.1 Lifestyle	64
	5.2 Risk	67
6	**Conclusion**	**71**
	References	**75**
	Further reading	**76**

1 INTRODUCTION

In Chapter 1 of this book Steve Hinchliffe and Judith Greene discussed the way in which our *natural* biological make-up interacts with the kind of *social* circumstances in which we live to produce both similarities and differences between individuals. We saw that there are complex interactions between what society provides and what we can do ourselves as agents. All of this was illustrated with reference to intelligence and child development.

As one of the authors of this chapter, and as an asthma sufferer, I am only too aware of how my biology interacts with my social and physical environment so that I avoid certain activities and certain places. However, despite taking care, I sometimes get a full-blown attack and this affects my ability to take part in my normal everyday activities. So it is of key interest to me what causes asthma and what might be the best way for me to deal with its effects. Is it primarily a biological condition that I can only hope to control with drugs? Is it a condition brought on by the urban environment in which I live? Is it exacerbated by the fact that I smoke? Controlling my asthma requires constant medication, so my 'illness' has a cost on the health service. Therefore, dealing with my asthma and that of other sufferers is of interest not just to me, but also to the government and indeed to everyone who pays for and utilizes the health service. So, looking at the causes of health and illness and possible interventions offers another way in which we can explore how the natural interacts with the social conditions in which we live.

Health seems to play an increasing role in our everyday lives. It is difficult to pick up a newspaper or magazine, listen to the television or radio, or visit a bookshop without being confronted with information on health or exhortations to avoid certain foods, take certain vitamins or minerals, take regular exercise and a host of other things. It seems that everyone is concerned with health – not just doctors and health care professionals, but the government, the media and indeed all of us who each year make resolutions to eat more healthily, drink or smoke less and take regular exercise. A lot of this information and advice seems to suggest that we can influence the extent to which we enjoy good health through the food we eat, the exercise we take (or don't take), the 'good' or 'bad' habits we have. In other words, we each seem to be responsible for whether or not we enjoy full, active, healthy lives.

Make a note of the sources of information and advice on health that you have come across. Which ones do you take particular note of?

Think about what you do to take care of your health.

FIGURE 2.1   The official line: government advice on the healthy life

However, despite this rhetoric of responsibility for oneself and one's health, a close look at the same sources tells us that atmospheric pollution is a major problem of the era and that it is largely responsible for breathing difficulties such as asthma in our cities. The 1990s also witnessed widespread concerns about the health effects of genetically-engineered food and saw heated debates about just how 'natural' the fruit and vegetables in our shops and supermarkets are. Increasingly, too, we hear about the medical discoveries of genes which play a part in the development of diseases such as cancer, whilst drug companies constantly seem to produce new treatments for many forms of disease. Many sources also suggest that feelings of being uneasy with ourselves and the stresses and strains of everyday life cause many illnesses. These arguments seem to suggest that there are many causes of illness which are not within the individual's control.

FIGURE 2.2 Take a deep breath – the pleasures of the motor car?

So, who or what is responsible for our health? Is it a matter of luck as to the kind of body we happen to have been born with? Is it to do with our lifestyle, our social or physical environment or the technology typical of Western industrialized societies? These are important questions. As individuals we are concerned to maximize our own health. However, these issues are also important for society as a whole. Apart from moral reasons for maximizing the health of the nation, provision of health services places a considerable financial burden on taxpayers. In Britain, around 7 per cent of the Gross Domestic Product (an indicator of the nation's income) is spent on health care services, whilst working time lost through illness places pressure on business and other organizations.

Most of us when we are ill consult a doctor. In the UK, each of us is entitled to register with a general practitioner who, if it is felt appropriate, can refer us on to a specialist or a hospital. This network of health services, paid for by taxpayers, but free at the point of usage, was set up in 1948 with the establishment of the National Health Service in the UK, which replaced a patchwork of private, co-operative and charitable arrangements. At that time, there was considerable optimism that free access to medical services would transform the health of the nation and clearly there have been considerable successes; life expectancies have increased, neonatal death rates and deaths from childhood illnesses have fallen. However, since the 1970s there has been increasing uncertainty about the power, by themselves, of medicine and conventional doctor- and hospital-based health services to maximize health.

This chapter traces the history of the growth of this uncertainty about how we should seek to improve the health of people in Western industrialized societies. In particular, we will examine how different conceptions of health and illness lead to different ways of seeking to maximize health; and how different forms of evidence have encouraged a more diverse explanation of how to improve health. During our historical tour we shall see how some explanations place emphasis on the role of structural features of our bodies or society whilst others are more concerned with the role that individuals play in making healthy choices.

The primary concern of this chapter is of course to examine how natural and social factors impact upon our health. Clearly, biological factors are important since none of us is born with a perfect body. The influence of biology in relation to health is most clearly stated in medical views of health and illness, so it is with an examination of just how medicine understands health and illness and how it conceives of the best method of treatment that we will begin.

SUMMARY

Working on this chapter will help you to:

- understand and give examples of different conceptions of health and illness;

- understand and describe the growth of uncertainty about how to maximize health and give examples of the more diverse approaches that have been proposed;

- understand how natural and social factors interact in health and illness;

- understand and give examples of the interaction of structural features and individual choice in health and illness.

2 'NATURAL' EXPLANATIONS: MEDICAL CONCEPTIONS OF HEALTH AND ILLNESS

For many of us, ideas about health and illness are largely derived from orthodox Western medicine. In our society, doctors are seen as *experts*. They advise us on how to avoid certain illnesses, diagnose us when we are ill, and devise and deliver the best treatment. To many of us this way of thinking about health and illness is 'natural', in other words, it isn't usually open to argument. But, beliefs about what health and illness are and what makes us ill have changed over time in our own society, are different in other societies, and indeed, as we shall see, vary between different groups in our own society. Thus, health and disease are what social scientists call **contested concepts**.

Contested concepts
Ideas over which there is basic disagreement, where meanings are not stable and where there may be social differences, debates and conflict.

What this means is that there is no one 'right' way of understanding health and illness. Now this does not mean that any explanation will do or that they are all accorded equal status. Rather, it suggests that we need to understand the different origins, language and logic of different health beliefs and examine the evidence which supports their claims and concerns.

Medical explanations of health and illness are based on particular views about:

- the relation between our bodies and our minds;
- what health and illness are;
- what makes for effective understanding.

2.1 The relation between the body and the mind: notions of health and illness

Until the seventeenth century, the soul and the body were seen as inextricably linked. Thus, conceptions of life and death, health and illness could not be separated from considerations of faith, sin and salvation. However, in the seventeenth century the philosopher René Descartes (1596–1650) challenged this view. He proposed that there were two kinds of what he called 'substances' in the world. The first is the mind, and the second is matter. In his view, mind is purely consciousness and doesn't take up space in the world, whilst matter (e.g. the body) does take up room in space. Thus, mind and body are subject to different forces. Spiritual forces act on the mind, but these are quite separate from the physical forces which operate on the body. This separation, or **dualism** as it became known, made it possible to

Dualism
An understanding which suggests that one idea or process is defined in relation to what it is not. A system of understanding based on opposites.

understand the human body quite separately from spiritual or religious concerns. Furthermore, while only humans have matter *and* minds (Descartes viewed other living things as consisting purely of matter), our bodies are nevertheless subject to the same physical forces which operate on the bodies of other living creatures and can be expected to work in a similar way.

Alongside these philosophical changes there were many important medical advances, especially during the nineteenth and twentieth centuries. For example, there were technical advances such as the stethoscope that marked a change in the way doctors interacted with their patients. Prior to this, doctors had to rely very much on what patients reported and what they felt was wrong. But the stethoscope allowed doctors to 'see inside' the patient and make their own observations of the body without having to rely on what the patient said or on outward signs of illness such as coughing. Pioneering laboratory experiments by people such as Pasteur found that some illnesses were due to micro-organisms entering

FIGURE 2.3   René Descartes (1596– 650) (engraving by W. Holl, after a portrait by Frans Hals)

FIGURE 2.4   A sixteenth-century anatomical dissection in Fabricus's anatomical theatre, Padua, Italy

the body. Together, these advances encouraged a view of illness as located within the biology of the body, with distinct causes which could be discovered by the doctor without the patient's help. Combined with the philosophical separation of the body and the mind, the way was cleared for doctors to see the study of the body as part of 'nature', subject to the same kinds of forces as other animals and amenable to study in similar ways. This mind and body dualism is analogous to, and works in tandem with, the separation of society and nature as pure opposites (see the Introduction to this book).

Descartes' view of the body is that it is essentially like a machine. Good machines tend to have many component parts working in concert to perform particular tasks. So, the ideal 'body' became linked with the idea of a well-oiled machine in which all the parts work together in harmony. When machines are working well or 'normally', we don't tend intervene. Only when they break down do we send for the mechanic or service engineer. So too doctors tended to be less interested in our bodies when they were working normally and usually only became involved when they 'broke down' or worked 'abnormally'. Over the years, doctors have sought to identify the causes of our 'machine' breaking down and to find ways of 'fixing' it. You will not be greatly surprised then to discover that doctors frequently have some difficulty in defining health and tend to define it in negative terms as the absence of disease.

FIGURE 2.5
The body as a machine: a contemporary image from a children's reference book

2.2 Effective understanding

The conception of illness as due to biological forces, and the ability to diagnose illness without the involvement or influence of the patient, gradually encouraged medicine to take on board the methods of the natural sciences which were transforming other aspects of our world in the eighteenth and nineteenth centuries.

Scientific methods are characterized by the systematic study of events. Complex entities like the body are broken down into manageable parts such as organs that can be observed and measured by the physical senses. Since particular organs such as the heart serve the same function in everyone's body, then in principle all hearts operate in the same way, so it doesn't matter who makes the measurements. Furthermore, hearts are assumed not to influence or be influenced by the act of observation. These assumptions have important implications. First, they allow measurements to be independent: in principle everyone who makes a particular kind of measurement will come up with the same answer. Second, they allow doctors to build up understanding of the parts and to discern regularities and patterns in illness which can be expressed as law-like universal statements. Medicine thus came to see itself and be seen by others as the accumulation of 'facts'. The strength of such understanding lies in the notion that the observations are not affected by the observer – they are said to be objective, and so they can be reproduced time after time allowing us to be pretty sure of our findings. It is this which has helped scientific medicine to become the most prominent way of understanding health and illness in our society. Indeed, it is often contrasted with other ways of understanding. For example, the British Medical Association describes it thus: 'In as much as scientific medicine lays such a firm emphasis on observation, measurement and reproducibility, historically it has become inevitably and increasingly separated from doctrines embracing superstition, magic and the supernatural' (BMA, 1986, p.61).

The many medical advances of the twentieth century provide ample evidence for the success of the medical model. Through the understanding of the microbiological processes of the body and how it fights disease, vaccination programmes such as that for polio have more or less eliminated the disease in Europe and North America. The scientific method has also allowed individual doctors to combine their knowledge with pharmacologists and chemists and so produce important treatments for common diseases. For example, heart attack is one of the most common causes of death in Europe. Over the years, individual doctors utilized a variety of drugs and treatments to help minimize the effect of the attack and to prevent death. However, because of this diversity in treatment, nobody really knew which was best. In the 1980s, a group of doctors in Oxford organized an international study to compare two of the most popular drugs. By looking into the body, it had been discovered that heart attacks are caused by blood clots getting stuck in the arteries of the heart. Blood cannot get through the arteries and a heart attack ensues.

Chemical analysis of a particular chemical compound demonstrated its action of effectively 'thinning' the blood. Thus, giving this compound to someone having a heart attack was hypothesized to help get the blood flowing around the heart again, thereby reducing damage. Patients entering hospital with a heart attack were randomly allocated to either drug A or drug B and their progress was monitored. The results revealed that the patients on drug A were very much more likely to survive. The results of this study were published and, within a few years, the drug was used by almost every doctor in Europe and North America and had substantially reduced the number of deaths due to heart attack. The name of drug A was aspirin.

It was these positive effects of widespread application of the medical model of health that created much optimism in the middle of the twentieth century. The establishment of the National Health Service had resulted in people no longer being required to pay doctors directly, so it was thought that this would permit health to become a reality for everyone in society, not just the well off.

From the description above we can see that medicine has a very clear view on 'nature'. For doctors, health is intimately related to our biological nature. Whilst aspects of our biology are specific to our species, it is nevertheless understood that biological processes operate in a very similar way in both human and non-human animals. We can best understand how our biological 'nature' operates in health and illness by adopting the same kind of method that scientists studying non-human animals employ. This scientific method has considerable power to aid our understanding of not just the causes of illness, but also of how illnesses should be treated.

It is also clear that doctors place more emphasis on structural factors than individual choice in their explanations of health and illness. Doctors do not completely reject the impact of individual choice; for example, they exhort us to stop smoking, to reduce our fat intake and to drink in moderation. However, when it comes to understanding the causes of health and illness and how best to organize treatment, they emphasize the biological *structure* of the body. The health choices we make in our everyday lives are of importance for our health only insofar as they affect that biological structure.

SUMMARY

According to the medical explanation of health and illness:

- the mind is separate from the body;
- the body is like a complex 'machine';
- illness is located in the biology of the body;
- knowledge and understanding are achieved through scientific investigation.

3 SOCIAL EXPLANATIONS: THE IMPACT OF SOCIAL CLASS

The dominance of medical views of health and illness was enshrined in the structure and practice of the National Health Service. There was considerable confidence that an objective medical profession would harness the power of modern science and technology to cure many if not most of the common illnesses and, as we noted in Section 2, there were many successes. Furthermore, since access to medical services would be determined by need rather than ability to pay, it was hoped that the overall health of the nation would improve.

However, considerable blows to this optimism occurred with the publication of two important government reports – 'The Black Report' in 1980 and 'The health divide' in 1992. The groups who produced these reports collected and analysed information about the relationship between social class and health. They looked at various statistics that purport to monitor the state of the nation's health. These include mortality (death rates), morbidity (illness rates) and life expectancy statistics.

Infant mortality is often taken as an indicator of the state of a nation's health. This is often expressed in terms of the infant mortality rate which is the number of babies who die per 1,000 live births. During the second half of the twentieth century, there appeared to have been considerable success in reducing infant mortality in Britain. In 1950, there were 31 infant deaths for every 1,000 live births, but by 1980 this figure dropped to 12 and in 1990 the figure was only 8 (*Social Trends*, 1992). This seems to suggest that the National Health Service was having a profound effect and its hopes of reducing 'needless' deaths were being fulfilled. However, a closer look at the figures indicates that babies who die are not randomly spread across all groups in society. Rather, analysis of the figures suggests that certain babies are more at risk.

ACTIVITY 2.1

Look at Table 2.1 overleaf which compares infant mortality in 1978–79 with 1992 in relation to social class.

1   How did infant and perinatal mortality change between 1978 and 1992?

2   Given the general trend, what are the differences between the social classes?

Social class is defined by the Registrar-General for England and Wales in the following way:

   I   Professional (for example lawyer, doctor, accountant)

   II   Intermediate (for example teacher, nurse, manager)

IIIN Skilled non-manual (for example typist, shop assistant)

IIIM Skilled manual (for example miner, bus driver, cook)

IV   Partly skilled manual (for example farm worker, bus conductor)

V   Unskilled manual (for example cleaner, labourer)

Other   Armed forces and economically inactive

TABLE 2.1   Perinatal and infant mortality rates per 1,000 total births 1978–79 and 1992 compared by social class (for marriage births only)

Social class	Perinatal		Infant	
	1978–79	1992	1978–79	1992
I	11.9	6.3	9.8	5.0
II	12.3	6.1	10.1	4.6
III (non-manual)	13.9	6.8	11.1	5.5
III (manual)	15.1	7.0	12.4	5.6
IV	16.7	7.4	13.6	5.8
V	20.3	8.9	17.2	7.9
Other	20.4	10.2	23.3	10.5
Ratio of social class V:I	1.71	1.7	1.8	1.6

Note: Perinatal deaths are those occurring during the first 28 days, infant deaths are those occurring between 28 days and 1 year.

Source: Oppenheim and Harker, 1996, Table 4.2, p.79

COMMENT

By looking across the *rows* in the table we can compare the rates for 1978–79 and 1992 in each social class. Thus, for example, we can see that for social class I the rate of perinatal death declined from 11.9 to 6.3, and the rate of infant death from 9.8 to 5.0. If you look at each row you will see that this reduction is repeated in every case. We can therefore say that this table shows a reduction in all deaths of babies during the period between 1978–79 and 1992.

However, if we now look at the *columns* in the table, we can see that in 1978–79 the rate of perinatal deaths showed an increase across the social classes from 11.9 in social class I to 20.3 in social class V. If you look at each column you will see that this story or 'trend' is repeated for both 1978–79 and 1992. Thus, children born to parents in social class V appear to be at more risk of dying than do the children born to parents in social class I.

Other analyses show that deaths are highest for babies whose mothers are under 16 or over 35. The majority of babies who die during the first year are also those who have a low birth-weight. Low birth-weight is associated with mothers who are less well off. So, it would seem that babies of young mothers who are poor are starting off life with a disadvantage. Even more sadly, the disadvantage of being born into the lower social classes seems to continue throughout the life course.

ACTIVITY 2.2

Look at Figure 2.6. Figures 2.6(a) and 2.6(b) show, respectively, the **standardized mortality ratio (SMR)** for men and women in Britain by social class for the years 1979–83. Figure 2.6(c) shows the infant mortality rate in England and Wales in 1990. Using SMR allows us to show the impact of social class on mortality rates An SMR of 100 is average for the population as a whole: under 100 indicates lower than average chances of death; over 100 higher than average chances.

Standardized mortality ratio (SMR) Standardized mortality ratios are a statistical device which allows us to compare the death rates of differently sized groups of the population by excluding all other factors, in this case keeping only class.

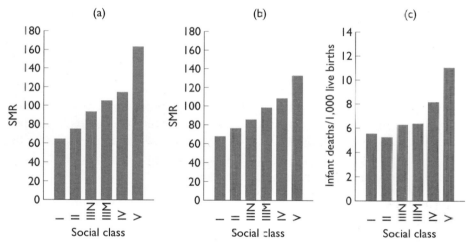

FIGURE 2.6   (a) Adult (20–64) male mortality rates, by social class, Britain, 1979–83; (b) Adult (20–59) female mortality rates, by social class, Britain, 1979–83; (c) Infant mortality rates, by social class, England and Wales, 1990
Source: Whitehead, 1992, Figure 1, p.230

How would you describe the relationship, if any, between social class and health expressed in this evidence?

COMMENT

The relationship between adult male and female mortality rates (as a proxy for standards of health) and social class is unambiguous. The poorer you are, the lower down the social scale you are, the shorter your life expectancy and thus the more likely you are to die, say, in your forties and fifties. In the case of infant mortality, the overall relationship between social class and mortality is the same, with increasing mortality rates in classes III to V, although the trend is not so clearly established in classes I to III.

During the period between 1950 and 1980 mortality rates for adults in social classes IV and V remained the same but there was a marked improvement in mortality rates for people in social classes I and II. Indeed, there is a clear and persistent social gradient in mortality rates at all ages. Of the 66 major causes of death, 62 are more prevalent in social classes IV and V than in other social classes. Rather than diminishing, it appears that class differences in health chances are increasing. Whitehead summed up these findings in 'The health divide' by saying that 'diseases of affluence have all but disappeared and what is left is a general health disadvantage of the poor' (Whitehead, 1992, p.232).

This rather depressing picture is supported by various surveys of people's self-perception of their health which indicate that people in the higher social classes are far more likely than those in the lower social classes to state that they are in very good health. Morris (1995), who was a member of the 'Black Report' working group, reflecting on the findings ten years later, said that when the figures were first established they came as a shock. Although there had been differences in the life chances of the well off and the less well off ever since statistics had begun to be collected, it had been hoped that the National Health Service and the welfare state would reduce the difference. It was a shock to find that, despite 30 years of ever-increasing expenditure on the NHS, despite the many advances in medicine, there were certain groups within society whose health had not improved. In seeking the reasons for this disparity, the working group pointed to the material conditions of life – income, housing, work and general environments.

Like medical explanations, analyses of health and illness which focus on social factors place emphasis on structural features rather than individual health choices. However, in contrast to medical explanations, it is the structural features of *society* rather than the body which are emphasized. For example, an association between poor housing and poor health has been described since the earliest studies in the nineteenth century. While housing conditions have generally improved since this time, evidence still suggests that they are a powerful factor.

There is evidence that other matters may also be important. Various studies were undertaken during the 1990s of Bangladeshi and Somali families who were classified as homeless and living in poor quality temporary accommodation in Tower Hamlets. They were subsequently resettled in new housing in Stepney and the Isle of Dogs. More than a year after resettlement, most families achieved a higher score on a health profile survey than they did on the same profile before the move. The reasons identified for this by the families were largely concerned with racial harassment which they said made them fearful and forced them to live restrictive lifestyles in which 'we feel like prisoners in our own homes' (Collard, 1996, p.24).

SUMMARY

According to social explanations of health and illness:

- Health and illness are not purely biological or purely social.
- The social and the biological interact to produce particular consequences for health.
- Social analyses of health and illness drew attention to the need for restructuring the economic and physical resources of society, but did not challenge the centrality of medicine in delivering health care services.

4 COMPLEX INTERACTIONS: THE COMPLEMENTARY HEALTH MOVEMENT

So far, you may have noticed that both the medical and social analyses we have examined have talked little about health and more about illness – what causes it, how to avoid it and how to treat it. Increasingly, however, various influences combined to challenge this rather negative view which emphasized illness and began to focus more on a positive concept of health. This also marked a move away from approaches that focused on things which people share in common, such as biological endowment and social class, and an increasing emphasis on personal factors, especially the way in which we lead our individual lives. The first of these influences which we will investigate stems from what has come to be known as the complementary health movement.

There has been a considerable change in our attitude to the place of non-orthodox therapies. Only a few decades ago, therapies such as acupuncture and homeopathy were regarded as really strange, but now, if the evidence from magazines and other media is to be believed, such therapies command considerable respect. Think of the variety of herbal remedies, aromatherapy oils and so on commonly available in local chemists. A huge variety of non-orthodox therapies is now available. Some, such as Chinese acupuncture, arise from traditions whose historical origins lie further back than do those of Western medicine, whilst others, such as guided imagery, are of more recent origin. Some, such as chiropractic or osteopathy, require lengthy periods of training resulting in registration as a practitioner, whilst others, such as aromatherapy, do not.

In the 1970s, these therapies were often referred to as 'alternative' therapies, in line with that decade's discussion of 'alternative lifestyles' and notions of a rejection of mainstream values by various groups of people. More recently, however, alternative therapies have gained new respectability, with many major public figures endorsing their use. It is now more common to see the term 'complementary' used by many approaches to signify that they do not reject medical diagnoses and that their techniques can be used comfortably alongside conventional medical treatment – for example, chiropractic therapy utilizes conventional anatomy and physiology. Others, however, seem to warrant the 'alternative' label. For example, homeopathy is based on the principle of treating like with like. Practitioners treat individuals with very small quantities of substances which excite similar symptoms in healthy persons to those experienced by the person who is ill, on the grounds that this stimulates the body to heal itself. This contrasts with most conventional medical treatment, which is based on the principle of allopathy, whereby illnesses are treated by drugs whose effects oppose the action of the disease.

It is difficult to estimate the size of the complementary sector since there is no single body like the National Health Service to enable the collection of statistics on numbers of practitioners, patients, frequency of consultation and so on. However, a number of studies have indicated that over the last few decades there has been an increase in the use of non-orthodox therapies and in the number and range of practitioners. In 1995, The British Medical Association estimated that one in four of the population of Britain had consulted a non-orthodox practitioner.

ACTIVITY 2.3

Have you consulted a complementary therapist? If so, why?

Even if you haven't gone to a therapist, have you used complementary aids to health such as aromatherapy? Why?

If you haven't used any form of complementary therapy, write down your reasons why not.

COMMENT ────────────────────────────

Compare any reasons you may have given for using complementary therapy with those that Ursula Sharma (1995) found in her study of the use of complementary therapies. She found that the reasons people gave for using complementary therapy fell into five groups:

- A view that conventional medicine failed to get at the 'root' cause of chronic illness or to take a preventative approach, treating the symptoms only.

- Fear of drugs becoming habit-forming or having unwelcome side-effects.

- Fear or dislike of treatments considered too radical or invasive.

- A perception that medicine failed to cope with social and experiential aspects of illness.

- Dissatisfaction with the doctor-patient relationship which gave the patient little control.

We can see from these statements that some of the elements of the medical approach to health and illness are no longer regarded as positive by some people. For instance, the medical approach of breaking the body down into parts has lead to a perception that it doesn't deal with the root causes of illness but only the symptoms. By treating the body as a biological 'machine' to be treated 'objectively', people feel doctors don't understand what it *feels* like to be ill and patients are treated as objects of diseases rather than individuals. Furthermore, rather than advances in surgery and drugs being seen as the panacea for illness, many are wary of the impact radical surgery has on their lives and of the possible side-effects of drugs.

To try to understand why complementary therapy appears to offer a positive alternative, we need to examine the underlying views about health and illness in complementary health in much the same way as we examined those for medical explanations.

4.1   The body and the mind: holistic approaches

In complementary health, the body and the mind are seen as vitally related to each other and to the environment. This leads to its description as a **holistic** approach. You will recall from Section 3 that the way in which the Bangladeshi and Somali families *felt* about their new lives impacted on their health. Thus, in contrast to medical explanations, which do not see the mind as directly influencing the body, this is a key characteristic of complementary therapies. Unlike traditional medical views, where our biological nature is something to be overcome or tamed, holistic approaches view nature as a rather more benign force. Most holistic therapies place much emphasis on the healing powers of nature and natural energies. In complementary therapy, nature, in all its forms – both internal in terms of biology, feelings and emotions and external in terms of the weather, seasons and other living things – is something to be embraced. The more we are in tune with these forces, the more healthy we will be.

Holistic
Holistic approaches promote ways of thinking that reject analytical or fragmented models of the world (i.e. the separation of the mind and the body) and look at component parts in combination, as a whole.

4.1.1   How health and illness are conceived

Holistic approaches argue that, in order to feel healthy, we need to find a balance of energies between our physical, emotional and mental aspects of health. Rather than breaking down bodies into parts, holistic approaches see

FIGURE 2.7 The Taoist Yin-Yang symbol of balanced opposites

things as connected and, ideally, in balance. The different forces that impact on us are neither positive nor negative in themselves, but rather finding balance is the key. No-one is either wholly ill or wholly well; even the dying may have good spiritual health. This approach applies to more than health. For example, male and female energies are seen as different, but, crucially, as balancing or complementing each other. Neither is complete without the other and both exist simultaneously in the same body. The Taoist Yin-Yang symbol is probably the best known version of this idea (see Figure 2.7). The circle of One encloses balanced opposites which contain within them small circles of their opposite.

Each one of us has innate healing energies and the way to achieve health and a sense of well-being is to liberate these energies. Thus, in contrast to Western medicine where the emphasis is on the doctor treating illness, the task of treatment in complementary therapies is to maximize the person's access to their own healing system. There is no real gap between the knowledge of expert and layperson – what people know differs, but all knowledge is valuable and individuals can enhance and harness their knowledge of themselves. In contrast to medical ideas that focus on ideas of the body as a machine, the metaphors used by holistic therapists are rather different. Rather than seeing themselves as something akin to a mechanic, they would see themselves as more akin to a gardener. The task of therapy is to create the right climate, to give support to natural growth processes recognizing that there are seasonal changes. We can see then that holistic approaches are concerned with balancing the various forces impacting on our lives. These include the forces of nature – both our biology and the larger environment – and the forces of social organization. Thus, inherent in this approach is the notion of the interaction of natural and social forces. Neither natural nor social forces are seen as primary, but rather it is the balance between them which is crucial. Note too that holistic approaches, with their belief in the integration of the body and the mind, believe that these forces interact with the individual and we must each take responsibility for using our choices appropriately to balance the particular forces impacting upon us at any one time.

ACTIVITY 2.4

What problems with medical explanations do complementary therapies respond to?

What alternatives do they generate? Jot down a few paragraphs under these two headings:

Medical explanations – problems

Complementary explanations – alternatives

COMMENT

Medical explanations – problems	Complementary explanations – alternatives
Dualism – separation of body and mind	Holistic – integration of body and mind
Focus on illness and cure	Focus on health, well-being and prevention
Emphasis on treating the illness	Emphasis on treating the person
Doctors as experts	Therapist facilitating individual to initiate their own change
Overcoming/taming nature	Harnessing nature's positive forces

4.2 Effective understanding

You will recall from Section 2 that much of the strength of the medical view of health and illness derived from its reliance on scientific methods. Many complementary therapies are not amenable to scientific study and hence have attracted considerable criticism from doctors and other scientists and some scepticism on the part of the layperson. Advocates argue, however, that lack of scientific support for complementary therapy is not so much a criticism of the therapies themselves, but of the nature of science itself.

Science relies on systematic observation by the physical senses. In conventional medicine, illness is caused by and resides in the physical body and can be observed by doctors. In contrast, holistic complementary therapies see health and illness as a complex interaction of physical, psychological and spiritual factors which are not necessarily amenable to external study by the physical senses. Medicine's emphasis on similarities between bodies also allows it to isolate particular diseases and devise specific treatments for those diseases which can be experimentally demonstrated to be effective. In contrast, complementary therapies stress that they treat the person rather than the disease. Thus, when you consult a complementary therapist you will be asked questions, not just about your illness, but about your lifestyle, diet, stresses, things which make you happy or sad, and so on. So, if two people both have the same symptoms, whilst a conventional doctor will probably prescribe a similar treatment, a complementary therapist might suggest very different treatments for each one, taking into account the different personalities, situations and lifestyles. This emphasis on individuality makes it almost impossible to run the kind of experiment (for investigating heart-attack treatments) described in Section 2.

However, this is not to say that complementary therapy is simply based on trust or faith. An increasing number of studies describe the physiological changes which occur as a result of such therapies. For example, studies of acupuncture indicate that the various acupuncture points have different electrical potentials and affect physical structures and processes such as neurotransmitters in the brain, breathing and the immune system. So, it is clear that acupuncture needles initiate physiological change. What is not yet understandable in terms of Western science is how particular configurations of acupuncture needles produce their effects.

Whilst these criticisms focus on what are seen as difficulties complementary therapies have in demonstrating that their treatments are effective, another set of criticisms challenges the notion of nature being a benign force. Just as healing, growth and renewal are a part of nature, so too are degeneration, decay and death. Whilst we might focus on the positive and this might contribute to preventing or delaying the onset of negative natural influences, nature, like the Yin-Yang symbol in Figure 2.7, contains both positive and negative forces.

SUMMARY

In the complementary health model:

- the mind is inextricably linked to the body;
- everyone has a healing potential;
- the task of treatment is to release this potential and restore the balance in 'natural' energies;
- treatment is aimed at the whole person and hence will be different for different people;
- it is difficult to demonstrate the efficacy of treatment.

5 THE NEW PUBLIC HEALTH: THE DECLINE OF ILLNESS AND THE RISE OF HEALTH

Around the time when complementary therapies began to gain popularity and some respectability, policy makers were also reassessing the best way to maximize the health of citizens of Western industrial societies. They too began to regard health and illness as the result of diverse forces which play themselves out in complex ways. A new direction in thinking about health was heralded in 1974 when the then Canadian Minister of National Health and Welfare, Marc Lalonde, proposed that there were four distinct elements to the causes of ill health (see Bunton and Macdonald, 1992, p.9):

1   inadequacies in health care provision;

2 lifestyle or behavioural factors;

3 environmental pollution;

4 biophysical characteristics.

This more complex approach to health and illness was taken up by many governments and by the World Health Organization and launched what has become known as the 'New Public Health'. This approach recognizes the diversity of influences on health, and places much more emphasis on the promotion of health rather than the treatment of illness. The 'new' definition of health was summed up in the Ottawa Charter for Health Promotion (1987) as:

> The process of enabling people to increase control over, and to improve, their health. To reach a state of complete physical, mental and social well-being, an individual or group must be able to identify and to realise aspirations to satisfy needs, and to change or cope with the environment … Therefore, health promotion is not just the responsibility of the health sector …
>
> (quoted in Davey et al., 1995, p.377)

This definition of health seems to encompass many of the factors affecting health that we have examined. Whilst acknowledging the importance of biology, it also includes social factors such as environmental pollution, adequate housing and diet, and psychological factors such as lifestyle choices. Furthermore, it shifts the view of health from an absence of illness to one that sees it as a sense of well-being. Note too that it indicates a more diverse responsibility for health. No longer are explanations couched in terms which emphasize either *structure* or *individual agency*, but rather, if we want to maximize both, then there must be action both at the level of the individual and at the level of society. It is the responsibility of health care professionals to provide adequate services and to advise people how best to make use of these services. It is the responsibility of governments to provide 'safe' and adequate environments, and it is the responsibility of individuals to choose healthy lifestyles based on sound information delivered by a variety of sources.

British policy makers were quick to take up this approach and in 1976 the Department of Health and Social Security published the document *Prevention and Health: Everybody's Business*. Whilst this ushered in policies which sought to improve social conditions such as housing, it also placed considerable emphasis on the individual's responsibility for maintaining health. The major focus was on fostering 'positive health' – in other words, to prevent illness and disease rather than to focus on treatment. The mass media were encouraged to 'market' health-enhancing behaviours such as eating healthily and taking regular exercise, whilst the government encouraged communities to develop health-enhancing environments such as providing local facilities like swimming pools and making access to exercise facilities more available.

Health promotion is directed not only at those who are sick, but also those who would regard themselves as well. For this reason, it cannot be confined to hospitals and surgeries, but has to move out into the community – to schools, workplaces, shopping centres – anywhere where people gather. In the past, attempts to improve health via community action were focused on *providing* services such as ensuring safe water supplies or adequate access to medical services. Nowadays, in a world in which we have access to many things that may have a negative impact on our health (for example, tobacco), the focus is more on persuading communities to provide circumstances which facilitate people making 'healthy' choices. Thus, to continue with the example of tobacco, as well as encouraging individuals not to smoke, many institutions have instituted 'no smoking' policies and provided employees with counselling and guidance on giving up.

Even from this brief account, some of the main lines of the New Public Health and its borrowings from other conceptions of health and illness can be discerned.

ACTIVITY 2.5

What appear to be some of the core principles of the New Public Health?

C O M M E N T _____

The core features of the New Public Health include:

- a positive and multidimensional conception of health and well-being;
- the view that health is something that is shaped by a combination of factors (social and biological; mental and physical; individual and collective);
- the view that health should be actively promoted by government, rather than focusing on curative medicine.

Two key components of the New Public Health are lifestyle and risk. This model of health acknowledges the importance of how people live their lives and the calculation of the risk which could be involved in particular lifestyles. We now look at these two aspects in more detail.

5.1 Lifestyle

Lifestyle
An integrated set of habits and practices, which both meet consumption needs and provide the basis for constructing social identities.

The New Public Health recognized 'lifestyle or behavioural' factors as a key element in promoting health and well-being. **Lifestyle**, like health, is a complex concept with different meanings in different contexts. In sociological terms it refers to the integrated set of routine practices and decisions we engage in every day in order to function in modern society; for instance, the way we dress, what and where we eat, how and where we socialize. But lifestyle has come to mean more than simply what we do. Anthony Giddens suggests that it has taken on a meaning in terms of who we *are*. He describes lifestyle as:

> ... a more or less integrated set of practices which an individual embraces, not only because such practices fulfil utilitarian needs, but because they give material form to a particular narrative of self-identity

> Lifestyles are routinised practices, the routines incorporated into habits of dress, eating, modes of acting and favoured milieux for encountering others; but the routines are open to change in the light of the mobile nature of self-identity. Each of the small decisions a person makes every day – what to wear, what to eat, whom to meet with later in the evening – contributes to such routines. All such choices (as well as larger and more consequential ones) are decisions not only about how to act but who to be.

(Giddens, 1991, p.81)

ACTIVITY 2.6

Let us stop for a moment and try to unpack the quotation.

Break it down into a series of distinct but interrelated claims and arguments.

COMMENT

1   Lifestyles can be thought of as a structured and routine pattern of social life – primarily acts of consumption, but also of interpersonal interaction.

2   Most of these acts – like eating or wearing clothes – have an obvious practical purpose. But to a considerable degree we have, in the West at any rate, choices about exactly how we do them.

3   The choices we make are also structured by questions of self-identity and personal narrative; our choices are shaped by the project of constructing a sense of who we are and who we are not in this world.

4   The repertoire of choices and patterns offered to us, the grounds on which we decide what are plausible or reasonable choices and combinations, is left open in this definition.

We can now think about changes in lifestyle using our own lives as sources of information. By adopting a particular style of dress, by buying particular kinds of food, reading particular magazines and so on, we are saying that we are a particular kind of person. In a sense, by adopting particular practices we *create* our identities (see **Woodward, 2000**).

Clearly, the creation of particular identities is associated with the consumption of particular goods and services. As you will see in Chapter 3, consumption emphasizes the individual's personal choice, and this is encouraged through 'lifestyle advertising' and 'style' TV programmes and magazines that help to define particular lifestyles and reassure us that the choices we make are reasonable and right. In relation to health, this approach emphasizes the achievement and maintenance of health as the responsibility of the individual. We are encouraged to monitor our own health and to develop healthy attitudes and behaviour.

We have seen that exhortations about healthy living don't just originate in the activities of state-sponsored health professionals, but also in a myriad of other sources from schoolteachers to supermarkets, the media and so on. There has also been an explosion of health 'resources' – be it goods such as health foods or exercise bicycles, or services such as fitness clubs and yoga classes in our local community. These affect every aspect of our lives. To take just one example, let's consider the foods we eat in the early twenty-first century.

ACTIVITY 2.7

Compare your diet now to the diet you had as a child. Think about whether there are differences in terms of the variety of foods you eat, and the way in which you prepare, cook and serve food.

Why have these changes come about? Did you change your diet consciously, prompted by information or advice of some kind?

COMMENT

Your answer to this question will vary according to your age, where you live and so on. However, our guess is that you will be eating a greater variety of foods than you did as a child, drawing on the foods of other countries and cultures. You may present your food differently now, taking more care to make it look attractive on the plate. Over the last few decades, changes in the way food is produced, stored and transported have resulted in a greater quantity and variety of foodstuffs being available all year round. We can now enjoy fresh strawberries at Christmas and we can choose between a number of different kinds, shapes and textures of tomatoes. In these circumstances, what we eat is a style choice influenced by vast numbers of cookery-books, nutritional guides and so on.

As you stand in the supermarket queue, think about what you can tell about a person's lifestyle by the kinds of food they have stacked in their trolley. We also seem to have more information about the food we eat. For instance, go to your food cupboard or freezer and take out any item of pre-packaged food. Read the label and see how, even on the most common of foods, various facts about the contents are listed.

A tin of baked beans contains more than beans! For example, a typical label lists beans, water, sugar, salt, modified cornflour, spirit vinegar, spice extracts and herb extract, and proudly claims on the label that it contains 'no artificial colours, preservatives or flavouring'.

Many writers suggest that a consequence of this emphasis on lifestyle is the notion that people are in control of their lives. They want to improve themselves and to attain or maintain good health. This view of contemporary society has important moral and political implications. It seems to suggest that we 'choose' our health through our lifestyle choices, rather than simply 'enjoying' it or 'having' it. So, rather than being something which is grounded in the structural nature of our biology or our society and thus in many respects, outside our control, health becomes a matter of individual choice and reflects our initiative, adaptability, balance and strength of will.

Several studies have demonstrated that attaining health seems to involve considerable effort. For example, when Crawford (1993) asked Americans 'Are you healthy? How do you know?', he found that good health is associated with self-discipline. When the interviewees talked about health, they included ideas like self-control, denial, discipline and willpower. They saw our current way of living as health-denying. We consume unhealthy products, lead a sedentary life, become addicted to harmful substances, and so on. Life in modern society is seen as inherently unhealthy and so to achieve health we have to exercise self-control. For these people, health is a state to be achieved and this goal competes with other goals in their lives and so it requires an active choice. If this is the view of health of ordinary people, then the next question seems to be, on what basis do we make our choices?

SUMMARY

- Behavioural and lifestyle factors contribute to the health of the individual and society.

- There is a mass of information available for people who wish to maximize their health.

- Contemporary life also allows us access to harmful substances and an unhealthy lifestyle.

- To attain health and a sense of well-being requires effort and self-control and the ability to make health changes.

5.2 Risk

Like health and lifestyle, **risk** also has a range of meanings. The term 'risk' derives from statistics and refers to the probability or mathematical likelihood of a certain event occurring (e.g. that one has a one in 14 million chance of winning a lottery). In this mathematical sense the concept of risk is neutral. It simply describes a situation. However, over time the term has taken on more ominous overtones so that risk is now seen as negative. There is a tendency to believe that – while unfortunate events do happen to us – if we know the causes *and* the chances of them happening to us, then we can attempt to avoid them. In other words, risk is viewed as a means to cope with

Risk
The statistical likelihood of a hypothetical threat or danger occurring. Risk has come to be associated with danger more than with chance.

uncertainty. In recent years, there has been a proliferation of so-called 'risk factors' associated with health – the idea of there being certain things we do or are exposed to that increase the hazard or threat of illness.

ACTIVITY 2.8

Make a list of all the risk factors to health that you can think of.

Consider which ones are within your control and which ones are not within your control.

COMMENT

If your list is anything like ours, then it will include certain behaviours such as eating red meat, drinking too much, smoking, not taking enough exercise. It might also include possible risks associated with preservatives or additives in food, or another set of factors such as toxins in water, increasing levels of ultraviolet light coming through the ozone layer, pollution from cars. In some ways, it would seem that almost everything we do carries with it some form of risk. Deciding just what the risk factors are, how we should assess them and how we should overcome them has become an important enterprise at the turn of the century. The reason for this emphasis on understanding risk factors seems to be to help us as individuals to predict disease and so try to gain some control over our lives. It also seems to help society to save money since, if risk factors are reduced, people are less likely to require acute and therefore expensive medical services.

We have already noted that lifestyle is now regarded as crucial to attaining and maintaining health and that this appears to suggest that individuals are in control of their lives. Thus, if individuals choose to ignore health risks, then they are placing themselves in danger of becoming ill. Illness results in them becoming less useful members of society and also incurs expense on the health service. As we saw above, attaining health is seen by many people to require effort and gradually this 'quest for health' has come to acquire moral overtones. Those who are overweight, smokers, lazy and so on are regarded as bringing diseases such as heart attacks upon themselves. 'Self-surveillance of bodily health', as Featherstone (1991) terms it, has become a part of contemporary lifestyles. But it has also become a way for certain classes of people to distinguish themselves from other classes. Ehrenreich (1990) says that the middle classes seek out activities and artefacts which mark their distinctiveness, such as membership of executive health clubs, or eating organic food. But executive health clubs are expensive. And whilst we have noted that food of all kinds is now more abundant in our supermarkets, the very forces which have contributed to this enhanced availability, abundance and range of food have also put pressures on food producers to produce fresh food which will endure long-distance transportation and arrive fresh and tasty. Thus, many foods have additives and preservatives which many fear are injurious to their health.

Increasingly, too, there is general alarm about the possible effects on health of genetically-modified foods. For these reasons, many have turned to 'natural', 'organically' produced foodstuffs. Ironically, however, these 'natural' foods tend to cost more than those that have been modified in some way. Those on fixed or low incomes may therefore be 'condemned' to eat less healthy and possibly harmful food.

The risks related to lifestyle, whilst frequently posed in terms of individuals' self-discipline and choice, can therefore be seen to be influenced by their structural position within society. Low income greatly restricts the lifestyle choices available and consequently the reduction in individual risk we are each able to make.

There also seem to be some risks which we, as individuals, find difficult if not impossible to control. The first of these are environmental risks. You will be looking further at these kinds of risks in Chapter 4 of this book, but for now let us note that the environment in which we live must allow us access to clean fresh water, clean air, shelter and a reasonable diet. Some theorists argue that affluence and overconsumption are leading us to destroy these aspects of our environment. To take just one example, the air in our cities has pollution levels that are higher than those recommended by the World Health Organization. Whilst traditional pollutants from industry and households have declined in Britain, we are now witnessing a new generation of problems. Carbon dioxide, methane and nitrous oxide are 'greenhouse gases' that are possibly contributing to climate instability. The long-term effects on health of such instabilities are difficult to assess but are likely to be profound. Meanwhile, another example is the depletion of the ozone layer which is likely to increase the incidence of skin cancer.

Whilst the New Public Health does not place sole reliance on medicine to maximize the health of the nation, nevertheless our biological characteristics and the role of doctors are still regarded as crucial. As health education has become more widespread, the media have played a vital role in 'educating' public opinion. Medical sections in newspapers, magazines and television programmes have become commonplace. Information is provided to make expert medical knowledge available to large numbers of people. Whilst for the most part this can be seen as a positive move, it does have some drawbacks. A subject which has attracted much media attention, but which exemplifies the dangers of oversimplification of the implications of risk reduction in the media, is genetic screening.

Although genetic screening has been available for many years, media interest was intensified when the Human Genome Project was initiated. This is a project designed to map the 1,000,000 or so genes that comprise human DNA, which is contained in every cell of our body. It is intended to identify every gene sequence in our body, and it is hoped that such identification might help us to understand genetic causes of a variety of diseases from mental illness to cancer.

But there are problems with much of this media coverage. It is not a simple matter of discovering *the* gene for cancer. Usually, diseases are caused by particular *sequences* of genes, and there are almost endless permutations of these sequences. In addition, as we saw in Chapter 1 of this book, social and environmental factors affect whether or not a particular genetic trait is expressed in the body. In other words, even though an individual might possess a particular gene or combination of genes, it doesn't necessarily show itself in the body without a particular social or physical environment. So genetic screening is not as simple as the media would often seem to suggest. It is not just a matter of identifying 'natural' forces, but rather one of understanding how these natural forces interact with forces in our physical and social environments.

Furthermore, as in the case of lifestyles, genetic screening carries with it serious ethical and moral issues for both individuals and for society as a whole. If screening reveals that someone possesses an 'undesirable' gene and that there is a likelihood of this gene being passed on to their children, then the individual has to make difficult decisions about whether or not to reproduce. Genetic screening also has the potential to detect the likelihood of contracting or developing disease later in life. This may be positive for the individual concerned, in that they may be able to change their lifestyle, diet and so on and delay onset. However, if this information is made more widely available, then the potential for serious problems ensues. If, for example, all new employees had to submit to genetic screening, they might be refused employment based only on the probability of them developing a disease at some stage. The late twentieth century witnessed the difficulties of those who have been tested as HIV positive and who often experience difficulty in obtaining employment, insurance and access to many aspects of life we all take for granted.

This oversimplified media coverage of genetic screening also has the potential to undermine the more diverse explanation of health that has gained ground in the late twentieth century. Genes are frequently described as 'coding' for particular functions or attributes, thereby reinstating the dominance of biological explanations without giving due account to individual choice, social and environmental factors. As we hope you will now appreciate, explanations that do not recognize and give due account to the diverse influences on health are unlikely to be satisfactory.

The above analysis makes clear that understanding risk and dealing with it is a very difficult business. It involves a complex mix of internal and external factors over which individuals have varying levels of control. The New Public Health model suggests that risk reduction is best enhanced by efforts to:

- encourage individuals to reduce their own health risks;
- support actions of organizations, communities, local, national and international governments to reduce external risks and provide conditions under which individuals can be encouraged to reduce their own risk.

But it must also be recognized that there are considerable difficulties, including:

- providing information in a way which enables individuals to make sense of the proposed risks;

- reorganizing society so that individuals can have equal access to risk reduction;
- presenting information on risk reduction in such a way that the existence of a probability does not exclude people from everyday activities;
- recognizing that action on environmental risk reduction must be orchestrated between societies as well as within individual societies.

SUMMARY

- The New Public Health model was a response to the limits of the social model.
- It introduced a much more multidimensional, multi-factor model of health.
- It draws on the notions of lifestyle and risk to make good some of the weaknesses in the social model.
- It alerts us to the importance of the external natural environment and pollution risks on health.
- It relies on risk assessment calculators whose claims are open to criticism.
- It advocates a less redistributive and more individualized, culturally focused set of health policies.

6 CONCLUSION

So what have we found out in our tour of conceptions of health and illness since the end of the Second World War? In particular, as the title of the chapter asks, *whose health is it anyway?* As one of the authors of this chapter, I began its exploration of health and illness by considering my asthma, asking what causes it and how best I can control it and reduce its effects on my everyday life. Let's explore this through the various explanations we have encountered.

ACTIVITY 2.9

Write notes in the grid overleaf on the emphasis each of the explanations we have examined would place on:

- natural or social explanations of asthma;
- whether managing it is within the individual's control.

	Medical	Social	Complementary	New Public Health
Natural/ social				
Individual control				

COMMENT

In the middle years of the twentieth century, medicine would have viewed asthma as primarily a natural condition – a result of my biological heritage. Thus, it was not within my control and so the best way of dealing with its effects was to hand myself over to doctors. Because doctors have at their disposal instruments and techniques to look inside the body and see how the physiological process of asthma works in lots of bodies, then they could run experiments to test for the best treatment. According to this medical view, all I really need to do is to comply with their instructions.

By the 1980s, social analyses prompted additional questions about the effect of social environments on the incidence of illness. These analyses, like those of medicine, looked for regularities, for patterns of health and illness in relation to particular social groups. Thus, asthma might be demonstrated to be related to, for example, damp housing conditions. If such an association was found, then pressure might be brought to bear on governments and housing associations to improve the standard of housing. Maximizing health in this approach was not aimed at the individual, but rather at improving conditions for everyone, with the assumption that this would improve health overall, and what residual illnesses were left over could best be dealt with by doctors. So if moving to a better home didn't cure my asthma, recourse to medicine and drugs was still seen to be the way forward.

Around this time, however, a variety of alternatives to drugs for dealing with asthma began to attract publicity. A huge number of different therapies were on offer – from acupuncture to aromatherapy, to herbs, to relaxation. Whilst doctors tend to define someone like me as an asthmatic, these complementary therapists would view me as a person with asthma. Instead of focusing only on the asthma, they would take into account a variety of other things about my life. In their view, asthma is not an inevitable result of either biological heritage or social environment. Rather, it is a result of an imbalance in the various physical, social, psychological, spiritual and environmental forces surrounding the individual. Some complementary therapists, such as acupuncturists, intervene physically to help balance those energies. Others, such as relaxation therapists, encourage meditation and making choices which encourage a sense of well-being. Such complementary approaches seems to accord the individual some control over his or her asthma, but the emphasis on the whole individual means that the evidence that complementary therapies produce for their efficacy cannot have the same degree of certainty as is provided by scientific explanations.

The New Public Health also seems to accord high value to balance and, like complementary medicine, suggests that conditions such as asthma are caused by complex interactions between biological, social and environmental, and individual factors. However, because it is primarily aimed at the level of policy, it looks for evidence which is based on regularities and patterns and so utilizes some of the techniques of the scientific approach. But it also accords some degree of control to the individual and seeks to provide social and environmental conditions which are conducive to health and which allow the individual to make sensible, healthy choices. In this view, asthma is neither a natural nor a social phenomenon, nor a result of entirely structural or individual factors. Rather, the boundaries between these polarized explanations have become increasingly blurred. Instead of focusing on which has the most power, research under the New Public Health is increasingly aimed towards understanding the way in which these interactions play themselves out in societies as a whole and within the individual. Considerable research has focused on identifying various risk factors to health which need attention, both by national and international governments and by individuals and groups. In this view then, my asthma is a complex interaction of natural and social forces and is affected by both structural and individual factors. Whilst the fact that I have asthma is not my 'fault', there are things I can do to reduce its effects.

ACTIVITY 2.10

To help you consolidate your understanding of each of the approaches to health which have been presented in this chapter, and to help you engage in the important task of comparing and contrasting them, have a go at answering the following questions by completing the table overleaf. Our notes are included at the end of the chapter to help you if you get stuck.

- What is the balance of natural and social forces in shaping people's health?
- How does each approach define health and illness?
- What does each see as the causes of health and illness?
- What are the implications for health services?
- What is the source of evidence for each approach?
- To what extent do individual choices and agency as opposed to social structures shape people's health?

	Medical approach	Social approach	Complementary approach	New Public Health approach
Emphasis on natural or social				
Definition of health and illness				
Causes of illness				
Implications for health services				
Sources of evidence				
Role of social structures and individual agency				

So it seems that there are lots of different ways of answering the questions as to who or what is responsible for our health. These different ways are based on different concepts of what health and illness are, and from these conceptions flow different ways of dealing with illness and promoting health. No single explanation seems to have all the answers. Each has its strengths and weaknesses. What is clear though is that health is a major concern both to individuals and to societies as a whole and research and investigation will continue in variety of spheres. What we hope you will be able to do as new ideas and evidence emerge is to view them critically, examining their basic assumptions, the kinds of evidence they produce, the kinds of explanation they offer and the kinds of intervention they suggest. We hope too that you will be alert to considering the possible ethical and moral issues they raise.

REFERENCES

British Medical Association (1986) *Report of the Board of Science and Education on Alternative Medicine*, London, BMA.

Bunton, R. and Macdonald, G. (1992) 'Health promotion: discipline or disciplines?' in Bunton, R. and Macdonald, G. (eds) *Health Promotion: Disciplines and Diversity*, London, Routledge.

Collard, A. (1996) *Homing In: Providing for the Health and Resettlement Needs of Rehoused Homeless Families*, Oxford, THHSG.

Crawford, R. (1993) 'A cultural account of "health": control, release and the social body' in Beattie, A., Gott, M., Jones, L. and Sidell, M. (eds) *Health and Wellbeing: A Reader*, Houndmills, Macmillan.

Davey, B., Gray, A. and Seale, C. (eds) (1995) *Health and Disease*, Buckingham, Open University Press.

Department of Health and Social Security (1976) *Prevention and Health: Everybody's Business*, London, HMSO.

Ehrenreich, B. (1990) *The Fear of Falling: The Inner Life of the Middle Class*, New York, Harper Perennial.

Featherstone, M. (1991) 'The body in consumer culture' in Featherstone, M., Hepworth, M. and Turner, B.S. (eds) *The Body: Social Process and Cultural Theory*, London, Sage.

Giddens, A. (1991) *Modernity and Self-Identity: Self and Society in the Late Modern Age*, Cambridge, Polity.

Morris, J.N. (1995) 'Inequalities in health: ten years and little further on' in Davey, B., Gray, A. and Seale, C. (eds).

Oppenheim, C. and Harker, L. (1996) *Poverty: The Facts*, London, Child Poverty Action Group.

Ottawa Charter for Health Promotion (1987) *Health Promotion*, vol.1, no.4, p.iii.

Sharma, U. (1995) 'Using alternative therapies: marginal medicine and central concerns' in Davey, B., Gray, A. and Seale, C. (eds).

Social Trends, London, HMSO (annual).

Whitehead, M. (1992) 'The health divide' in *Inequalities in Health,* Harmonsworth, Penguin.

Woodward, K. (2000) 'Questions of identity' in Woodward, K. (ed.) *Questioning Identity: Gender, Class, Nation*, London, Routledge/The Open University.

FURTHER READING

There is an enormous body work on health and illness in the social sciences.

Margaret Whitehead's edited collection *Inequalities in Health* (1992, Harmondsworth, Penguin) is the central point of reference for all debates around social explanations.

For an accessible and critical overview of complementary explanations, see Ros Coward's *The Whole Truth* (1990, London, Faber and Faber).

On the New Public Health and discussions of risk, an excellent overview is provided by Deborah Lupton's *The Imperative of Health: Public Health and the Regulated Body* (1995, London, Sage).

Michael Hardy's *The Social Context of Health* (1998, Buckingham, Open University Press) provides a useful introduction to the concerns of health psychology and includes an overview of the history of medical explanations.

COMMENT ON ACTIVITY 2.10

	Medical approach	Social approach	Complementary approach	New Public Health approach
Emphasis on natural or social	Natural	Social	More natural: mind and body viewed holistically	Both. Interrelationship between natural and social
Definition of health and illness	Emphasis on illness: health defined as absence of disease	Emphasis on illness	Emphasis on health	Emphasis on health, but recognition of importance of treating illness
Causes of illness	Biological factors	Social factors	Imbalance	Natural and social, exposure to risk
Implications for health services	Doctors, hospitals, 'experts'	Redistribute economic resources	Therapists as facilitators	Health responsibility of all: governments and business responsible for providing healthy environment, individuals responsible for making healthy choices
Sources of evidence	Scientific experiments	Statistical surveys	Personal efficacy	Risk assessments
Role of social structures and individual agency	Emphasis on biological structures and agency of individual doctors	Emphasis on social structures	Emphasis on personal agency	Combination of social and biological structures and individual agency, e.g. lifestyle and risk assessments

Nature for sale

Susan Himmelweit and Roberto Simonetti

chapter 3

Contents

1	**The 'natural' environment**	**80**
2	**Markets and the 'invisible hand'**	**86**
	2.1 The neoclassical theory of what markets do best	88
3	**Modelling markets**	**90**
4	**How prices are formed**	**92**
	4.1 State 1: No market	93
	4.2 Stage 2: Introducing the market	95
	4.3 Stage 3: Equilibrium prices	96
	4.4 A market with multiple sales	98
5	**Externalities and the 'invisible elbow'**	**100**
	5.1 Externalities	100
	5.2 The 'invisible hand' and the 'invisible elbow'	106
6	**Controlling the 'invisible elbow'**	**107**
	6.1 Power in the market	108
	6.2 The problems of valuing the environment	109
	6.3 Beyond the market	110
7	**Conclusion**	**112**
	References	**113**
	Further reading	**113**

1 THE 'NATURAL' ENVIRONMENT

As we discovered in the previous two chapters of this book, drawing the distinction between what is social and what is natural is harder than it first looks. We found social and natural factors to be inextricably connected in explaining both our personalities and our health. In this chapter we shall move outwards from ourselves to examine the natural environment, an aspect of 'nature' that apparently lies outside and is independent of us, and existed prior to human intervention. In doing so, we shall reflect the increasing concern in recent years about the destructive effects of human beings on the natural environment, and consider the interrelation of the social and the natural in creating such problems.

ACTIVITY 3.1

What do you mean by the natural environment? Take a few minutes to write down ten words that the term 'natural environment' suggests to you.

Our list includes a mix of different types of things. There are examples of non-human resources, such as forests and fish stocks, that, in the past, people tended to assume they could use as they liked; now there is concern that stocks are not being sufficiently replenished (see Figure 3.1). The environment, then, is something we can use up.

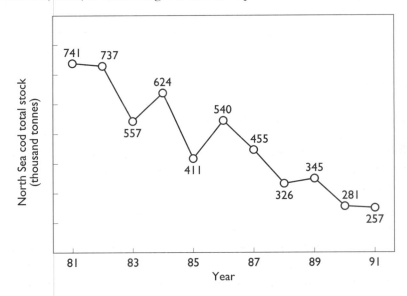

FIGURE 3.1   Fish stocks in the North Sea 1981–1991

Water and air are on our list too. They are there because they are important constituent parts of the context in which we all live our lives. We do not each have our own patch of clean air; we share the air we breathe and our water comes from a common source. The problem here is that the activities of a few people can contaminate such **shared resources** for everyone. We all breathe the same air and, unless we go to the expense of buying bottled water, depend upon the same water supplies. The environment, then, is something that we all share and can spoil for each other.

On our list we also have the climate and the beauty of unspoiled countryside. These are like clean air in that we all share the climate, but the climate seems to be subject to more long-term influences and changes more slowly. So, depending on which forecast of the effects of global warming you look at, our worries about the climate may be less about what will happen in our own life times, and more about the conditions under which future generations will live. The environment, then, is something that we can damage for the future.

The items on your list probably differ from ours, but we would be surprised if your list did not contain some similar examples of stocks that are being depleted, shared resources that are being spoiled and aspects of the world around us that we could damage for future generations. And, like our list, we expect that yours reflects current concerns. Our list does not include the stock of flies, for example, because we have not read of any serious concerns about diminishing stocks of flies and we are not particularly fond of flies ourselves. Similarly, although we all depend on the sun more fundamentally perhaps than anything else, our list does not include it as part of the environment. Though the sun is obviously an important shared resource that we do not want spoiled and without which future generations could not exist, we do not know of anything that people are currently doing that has been thought to threaten the sun in any way that would have serious consequences for us now or in the future. When talking about the natural environment, we tend to include only those areas of the natural world on which people are having or might have an effect, and where consequent changes may, in turn, adversely affect us. There are other approaches to the natural environment that are more ecological and less human-centred, but, in practice, our more human-centred or 'social' approach is used in most political debates about the environment. This is another example of where the natural and the social are inextricably intertwined, in this case, in what we even recognize as the 'natural' environment.

We have probably never been so aware of how our actions can damage the environment as we are now at the beginning of the twenty-first century. Interest in the environment has steadily increased over the last twenty or thirty years, and a number of 'green' organizations (from non-government pressure groups, such as Greenpeace, to influential political parties such as the German Greens) have ensured that governments that are keen to retain votes must address environmental issues.

Shared resources
Resources that are not privately owned by anybody and whose use is freely shared.

A number of factors lie behind the emergence of this green consciousness, including some large-scale environmental disasters provoked by human actions such as the deadly gas leak from the Union Carbide plant in Bhopal that killed thousands and left many more permanently disabled, and increasing worries about nuclear power since the Chernobyl disaster. Had you heard of Chernobyl before it sent a radioactive cloud over Europe and beyond?

Such environmental accidents have made people realize that human technology can have devastating and irreversible effects on the environment. However, many green organizations worry more about the less spectacular but more widespread environmental degradation that seems to accompany normal economic growth. The unprecedented economic growth that industrialized market economies, such as Britain, have experienced over the last two hundred years seems to have led not only to much higher levels of consumption, but also to the degradation of the natural environment.

ACTIVITY 3.2

Figure 3.2 is a line chart that illustrates the economic growth of the UK, the US and Japan from 1820 to 1989. The indicator used, GDP per person, roughly measures the amount of goods and services produced per person in a country.

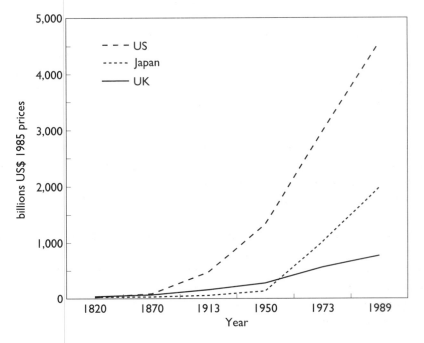

FIGURE 3.2   Economic growth in UK, US and Japan; GDP per person
Source: Maddison, 1991, Table A.2, pp.198

Each line in the chart tracks the value of **GDP** per person over time for the three countries – UK, US and Japan – from 1820 to 1992. (The 'legend' allows you to identify which country each line represents.) The lines rise for all countries over the years in the period considered, showing that **economic growth** has been a key feature of the last two centuries for these industrialized countries. You can see that the slopes of the lines become even steeper from 1950. This indicates that, on average, the increase in GDP per person was greater in the years since 1950 than in the years before it.

A similar picture emerges from Table 3.1 which reports the average yearly rates of growth for the same three countries over the same period.

TABLE 3.1   Economic growth in Japan, UK and US: average yearly rate of growth of GDP per person in selected periods (per cent)

Country	1820-70	1870-1913	1913-50	1950-73	1973-92
Japan	0.1	1.4	0.9	8.0	3.0
UK	1.2	1.0	0.8	2.5	1.4
US	1.3	1.8	1.6	2.4	1.4

Source: Maddison, 1995, Table 1-3, pp.23-24 and Table A-3a, pp.104-107

You can see from the table that, on average, growth was highest in the period between 1950 and 1973, when the yearly rate of growth has the highest value for all three countries (and especially for Japan, which shows an astonishing rate of growth of 8 per cent). It is not surprising, therefore, that many concerns about the effect of economic growth on the environment started emerging in the 1960s.

Most environmental degradation is not the result of anybody consciously deciding to pollute the atmosphere or run down fish stocks. Rather, when we talk about environmental degradation, we mean the unintended consequences of actions whose intended effects are quite different and may be wholly beneficial. When people have a primary purpose of creating harm we do not talk about it as environmental degradation, rather we see it as an act of vandalism or war. And, usually, governments have not set out to promote environmental damage. Most now claim to be committed to environmental protection and improvement. However, despite such commitments, the general consensus is that environmental degradation is getting worse not better.

Some unintended consequences are simply the result of ignorance. People did not know that certain gases, such as CFCs, might cause the problems that we now believe they do. But if ignorance was the only problem, then people would stop as soon as they understood the harmful consequences of their actions. The problem lies deeper, in that people, firms and states may even knowingly continue to cause environmental degradation, precisely because

GDP (Gross Domestic Product)
Measures the total quantity of goods and services produced in a country in a period of time (usually a year).

A country's economic growth
The expansion of a country's economy, which is often measured by the rate of change of GDP or GDP per person.

their primary purpose is elsewhere. Environmental degradation, then, is a regrettable by-product of their primary activities, but the imperative that drives those primary activities has much more force than concern for the environmental consequences. And this applies at all levels of society: whenever people drive to work because it is more convenient than taking public transport; whenever firms pollute rivers with their waste because it is cheaper than a cleaner production method; or whenever governments allow oil companies to despoil parts of the countryside because they fear the electoral consequences of raising direct taxes rather than relying on oil revenues. In all these cases, environmental degradation is a by-product of other actions carried out by people and organizations who, in their particular circumstances, do not consider avoiding the consequent environmental degradation to be worth abandoning their primary objective. For them, at least, the gains outweigh the losses.

In this way, environmental degradation has been the by-product of economic growth in the past and continues to be so in many ways, despite a greater awareness of environmental issues. Some see environmental degradation as the inevitable counterpart of economic growth; so that the only way to protect the environment would be to slow down or even cease economic growth. Others argue that environmental degradation is not an inevitable by-product of economic growth, but has happened because of the way economic activity is organized in modern industrial economies, and we could have sustainable economic growth that is environmentally friendly if we organized it differently. For them, the culprit is not growth itself, but the way growth is currently organized through markets.

Market forces
This refers to a characteristic of competitive markets, in which economic agents are not free to set prices and must buy or sell at prices given by the market.

Market economy
An economy in which resources are mainly allocated through exchange in markets.

In markets, people tend to look after their own interests and in doing so they neglect the environmental consequences of their actions. For example, environmentally safe methods of pest control, or at least ones that are much safer than those used today, have been available since the early 1960s. They are not applied because other environmentally less desirable methods of pest control are less costly and generate higher profits for the people who decide what pesticides to use. It is not that the people making these choices are inherently greedy. Rather, they have little choice. **Market forces** ensure that firms that do not choose the most efficient, that is the least costly and thus the most profitable, methods of production will not survive. This is because in competitive markets, firms with high costs can only sell without a loss if they set a high price, but buyers will not buy their products if more efficient competitors charge a lower price for the same item. So in a **market economy** it is no use appealing to people's better nature. Economic organizations, such as firms, have no choice but to choose the least costly methods of production – and so if some of the costs can be off-loaded onto the environment they will be. The market is a structure and the people and organizations that operate within it have to live by its rules – the rules of market forces – or die.

According to this argument, environmental degradation is not an inevitable consequence of growth in *all* circumstances, but of growth in an unregulated market economy. This suggests that there might be ways in which the economy can be changed and the action of market forces modified so that they work to protect rather than destroy the environment. Whether market forces can be modified to environmentally beneficial ends is a subject of intense political debate.

This chapter aims to give you some of the economic background to that debate. First we need to look at how the market works when it works well, so in Section 2 we examine how the argument could be made that a market allocates resources in the best possible way. Section 3 looks at how models can be used to investigate the ideas behind the theories and Section 4 goes on to investigate the model of the market using a worked example. In Section 5, in contrast, we look at why this model does not hold for all types of resources, including many natural resources, and what would need to be done to modify the operation of markets in these cases. This should leave you in a position, in Section 6, to assess the economic and political arguments for and against the idea that it is possible to modify or regulate a market economy so that it protects, rather than harms, the natural environment.

SUMMARY

- Environmental problems are generated at the interface of nature and society.

- Environmental problems include using up stocks of exhaustible resources, misusing shared resources and ignoring the interests of future generations.

- Historically there has been a link between economic growth and environmental degradation, at least in market economies.

- In such economies, the market is a structure within which people must operate. Sometimes they have little choice but to act in environmentally unfriendly ways if they are to survive in a market economy.

- This raises the question of whether markets can be modified in ways that would enable people to protect rather than harm the environment.

2   MARKETS AND THE 'INVISIBLE HAND'

In the previous section we raised the question of whether environmental problems were the inevitable by-product of economic growth in a market economy. By a market economy we mean an economy in which the main way in which resources are allocated is through markets. To answer that question we have to understand what is meant by a market and how markets allocate resources.

How would you define a market? What is the main activity that goes on in a market? What distinguishes one market from another?

You may have thought of local fruit and vegetable markets, big shopping centres or even car boot sales. In these cases, the idea of a market conjures up a physical place where many buyers and sellers come together to trade goods and services, exchanging them usually for money. *Exchange* is certainly central to the definition of any market. But to define the market as a place where goods and services are traded is too restrictive because there are many different ways in which exchange can happen, not all of which require buyers and sellers to meet in one place, for example we can buy a book by going to a local shop, by post through a catalogue or at home on the Internet.

FIGURE 3.3   Not all markets are like this local fruit and vegetable market where buyers and sellers meet in one place

Markets also differ according to what is exchanged; buying a second-hand car is very different from buying a pension or the services of a childminder. So we define a **market** by the commodity that is exchanged in it, and talk about 'the market' for second-hand cars, for pensions or for childcare. According to this definition, shopping centres are not markets, but places where parts of many markets operate. Markets can have geographical boundaries – we can talk, for instance, about the differences between the American and Japanese labour markets, but some markets have no boundaries – for example global markets exist for some commodities such as crude oil or copper.

A market
A market comprises all the exchanges involving a certain type of commodity (often within a defined geographical area).

A market consists of *buyers* and *sellers* that trade in its commodity; these are known as economic agents. An **economic agent** does not have to be an individual, it can be any entity that can come to a decision and act upon it; so organizations such as firms, households, charities and governments, as well as individual people, are economic agents. In order to trade, agents have to *interact* in some way, not necessarily face to face; networked computers, for example, are widely used in financial markets. Markets also need trading rules and conventions to regulate the way agents interact; these are social institutions that may vary between one market and another. However, one institution that is common to nearly all markets in a modern economy is the use of money. Instead of being directly exchanged (bartered) for each other, commodities are usually exchanged for money and have a price expressed in money terms. Money is a social institution that only works when people accept that it is exchangeable against all other goods and that it will not lose its value.

Economic agent
An entity, such as an individual, a firm or a government, that can make economic decisions and act upon them.

A sale results in the transfer of **property rights** in a commodity from seller to buyer. Property rights usually give owners the right to use and dispose of their property. However, there are some types of property where ownership does not confer both these rights. For example, without planning permission we cannot use houses we own just as we like. Other property cannot be disposed of, for example the properties that the National Trust owns are inalienable, this means that they cannot be given away or sold. In general, however, people have the right both to use their own property as they like and to sell it. If you do not want to use something that you own, it makes sense to exchange it with someone else who has something you do want. This is the rationale behind the propensity 'to truck, barter and exchange' that Adam Smith, the Scottish philosopher who is considered to be the founder of modern economics, saw as the basis of a modern economy.

Property rights
The rights of owners to use and dispose of their goods.

Markets also differ in the number and types of agents who trade in them. In some markets, such as telecommunications, only a few large companies sell goods and services, whereas in others a myriad of sellers compete without even knowing of each other's existence. In markets where there are many buyers and sellers, no single agent is likely to have much influence over what goes on. In particular they will not be able to do much about the prices at which they can buy or sell. It appears, then, that the market itself determines prices and therefore the possibilities that are open to buyers and sellers. All agents in such competitive markets feel themselves subject to market forces and will survive only if they are efficient. If there are few sellers in a market (or even only one) each seller will have power to influence prices, and market forces will not be quite so constraining. This is why governments usually regulate such markets, or try to promote competition in order to impose the discipline of market forces on monopolies. Similar problems arise in markets where there are few buyers.

SUMMARY

- In markets, agents exchange property rights over a commodity, usually for a price paid in money.

- Markets are defined according to the commodity exchanged (in some cases within a certain geographical boundary).

- An economic agent is any entity that can make economic decisions and act upon them. Governments, firms, individuals, charities and trade unions can all be economic agents.

- Markets in which there are many buyers and sellers are competitive. In such markets, no individual agent has much power and 'market forces' determine prices.

2.1   The neoclassical theory of what markets do best

Economists, from Adam Smith in the eighteenth century onwards, have praised the way in which markets have contributed to the achievement of greater human prosperity. In his book *The Wealth of Nations*, Smith introduces his famous 'invisible hand' as a metaphor for how markets work to co-ordinate the self-interested actions of agents to the common good.

Modern neoclassical economists, who form the dominant mainstream school in economics today, have continued Smith's work by trying to clarify the conditions under which markets work well and what benefits they deliver. In their view, one of the main benefits of markets is that, under the right conditions, markets will allocate existing resources to satisfy current human wants in the most efficient way. In this it is assumed that all important 'wants' can be satisfied by the consumption of goods and services, and generally that all 'resources' are privately owned. We will see later the extent to which neoclassical analysis can be applied to resources that are not privately owned and can be spoiled by current use or, like fossil fuels, are non-renewable. We look at whether this analysis can take account of 'wants' that cannot be satisfied by consumption.

The neoclassical view of the market focuses on how, in a market economy, choices made by vast numbers of economic agents, each following their own interests, result in goods and services being produced that make those choices feasible. It assumes that consumers, given their incomes and current prices, decide what to buy self-interestedly according to their tastes, without considering the wider effects of their actions. Similarly, firms decide what to produce and what resources to use according to what is profitable to them at current prices, given the technology to which they have access and the prices they must pay for the resources they use, again without considering any wider effects. Given this, how do markets ensure that all those decisions are co-ordinated efficiently so that agents, prepared to accept current prices, can find what they want to buy or sell? In the neoclassical view, markets alone can achieve an impressive degree of co-ordination through the working of the **price mechanism**.

Prices provide economic agents with incentives to use resources efficiently by collecting all relevant information and conveying it efficiently. If, for example, a bad harvest in Brazil leads to a shortage of coffee, there will be insufficient coffee available to satisfy all consumers who want to drink coffee at the existing price. Sellers then find they can raise the price of coffee and still sell it. Buyers experience a rise in the price of coffee and only those who are willing to pay more for it (either those who particularly like drinking coffee or have more money to spend) will now buy it. So when the price of coffee rises, consumers are given an incentive to consume less coffee and switch to drinking something else. This will result in less coffee being sold, but those customers willing to pay the new higher price will still be able to drink it – the price rises until it has persuaded just the right number to spend their money elsewhere and *all* customers willing to buy coffee at the new price will be satisfied. Similarly, if the price has risen only just the right amount, there will be no sellers left with coffee still to sell. Coffee consumption will be reduced without coffee drinkers needing to know the cause of the shortage.

So prices direct the allocation of goods towards those consumers who value them more, that is, those who are willing to pay more for them. Producers also look at prices in order to decide what and how much to produce. If the production of a good is not profitable because too few consumers want it and therefore the price is too low to make a profit, producers switch to the production of a good for which demand is high. If too many producers want to produce the same good, however, they will have to compete in order to win customers; they will do so by offering to sell at a lower price. If the price of coffee falls, for example, some producers will decide that it is no longer worth producing coffee; these will be the least efficient coffee producers, that is, those with the highest costs. In this way, the movement of prices ensures that coffee is produced by the most efficient producers, and drunk by those consumers who value it most.

All information about both the resources needed to produce a good (like coffee) and the value that consumers place on the consumption of that good is summarized in the price of the good. So, the price of a good reflects both the costs of the resources needed to produce it and the value that consumers put on its consumption. These producers and consumers might be spread out throughout the world and most will never meet each other, but the world price for coffee, for example, will reflect all these different conditions in a

Price mechanism
The way in which prices co-ordinate the actions of buyers and sellers in markets by providing them with information and incentives that shape their decisions, and the way in which all buyers' and all sellers' actions together determine prices.

single number. According to this account, the price mechanism enables markets to use all the relevant information available in the economy efficiently to allocate resources.

It is this ability of the market to co-ordinate the economy without the knowledge or intervention of people that led Adam Smith to talk about the price mechanism as if it was an 'invisible hand'. He was impressed by how an economy consisting of a myriad of producers all behaving in their own self-interest, that is, trying to make as much profit as possible without considering the effects on other people, did not collapse into anarchy. Instead there would be a functioning market in which customers could purchase whatever they wanted, provided they would pay the going price, and producers could sell all their goods at that price.

SUMMARY

- Neoclassical economists claim that the market allocates existing resources in an efficient way, by which they mean that goods are allocated to the consumers who are willing to pay most for them, and are produced by the most efficient producers, that is, those with the lowest costs.

- The price mechanism is central to the functioning of markets. Prices are determined by the interaction of consumers' and producers' decisions.

- Prices co-ordinate the actions of economic agents in markets by providing sufficient incentives and information on which agents can base their decisions. The final outcome of the decisions made by agents based on prices is an efficient allocation of resources.

- Adam Smith saw the price mechanism as the 'invisible hand' that allowed the market, without human intervention, to co-ordinate the behaviour of producers acting in their own self interest, in such a way that consumers' needs were satisfied.

3 MODELLING MARKETS

Model
A model is a simplified representation of reality in which only the essential elements of the social process under investigation are included.

The neoclassical theory of how markets work to allocate resources efficiently is an example of an economic **model**. It is not an easy task to describe how all markets work because markets differ in the type of commodity exchanged, in the trading rules that are observed and in the number and type of agents that participate in them. Nevertheless, all markets have some common characteristics and it is these that neoclassical economists have used to build their model of the market. In other words, they have selected some basic features that characterize markets and the behaviour of agents in markets to show how a simplified, ideal market works.

Model building is extensively used in social sciences to investigate social processes. Models are simplified representations of reality which focus on the features common to different instances of that process (in this case agents buying and selling in markets) and everything that is not essential to the understanding of the process under investigation is left out. When we build a model, we consider only the essential characteristics of the phenomenon studied; other characteristics that are deemed to be unimportant, that is, those that are thought not to influence the process examined, are left out. Which characteristics are important, in turn, depends on the specific purposes of the investigator.

Although we do not talk about them that way, we build models every time we try to explain any causal relationship. If I claim to have an explanation of how traffic fumes cause children's asthma, I mean that I have a general story that runs from some significant constituents of traffic fumes, through to a picture of how the human respiratory system works, to what produces the symptoms of asthma. However, you would not expect me to start my explanation by telling you how particles in the exhaust fumes of the number 37 bus ended up in a particular child's lungs and the effects that they had on her air passages before going on to list the effects of every other vehicle on every other child's breathing problems. You would expect me to talk about the connection between exhaust fumes in general and asthma in particular, that is, to build a model that simplifies in order to get away from the detail. In order to get away from the complex detail of reality, we have to try to find general features to characterize any particular process we want to understand and leave out the messy details from the picture.

In order to be useful, models have to be parsimonious – that is, composed of few elements and relationships. If a model is too complex, the basic processes get lost in the detail – it becomes a case of not being able to see the wood for the trees. However, models must still preserve all the fundamental characteristics necessary to understand the process being investigated. So, a model builder must strike a balance between simplicity and comprehensiveness.

Models can be expressed both in sophisticated mathematical notation and through everyday language. The neoclassical explanation of how the price mechanism works to allocate resources to satisfy consumers' wishes that you met in Section 2.1 was a model expressed solely in words, in which the movement of prices played a fundamental role. However, there was also a hidden simplifying assumption that there was a single price for each commodity. This in itself needs explanation; why should we expect to pay similar prices when we buy a particular good? Section 4 outlines a different type of model, one which uses a numerical example to illustrate the process by which a market arrives at a single price for a commodity. The model also shows why that price can be seen as the 'right' one for the commodity, given the particular characteristics of buyers and sellers in the market.

S U M M A R Y

- A model is a simplified representation of reality used to understand causal relationships within social processes.
- A model should leave out everything that is not seen as essential to the process under investigation.
- Models must be simple enough to be understandable and comprehensive enough to include all the features relevant to explaining the process being investigated.

4 HOW PRICES ARE FORMED

The model in this section is designed to illustrate how prices are formed. It looks at a market for a good that doesn't differ in its quality, and in which there are just five potential producers and five potential consumers. Because it is convenient to give the good a name, we'll call it a loaf of bread. We know that, in practice, loaves of bread differ in all sorts of ways, but those in our model do not. Ignoring the different qualities of the bread is a simplification that is designed to aid our understanding, but sufficient complexity is left in our model in order for us to learn about the price mechanism.

For the price mechanism to work, producers and consumers must differ among themselves. Some producers can produce a loaf of bread more efficiently and thus more cheaply than others. Perhaps the more efficient producers use newer machinery or have a more skilled workforce, or perhaps they are only more 'efficient' because they use a cheaper sort of wheat that is produced using some environmentally undesirable pesticides. For whatever the reason, their **unit costs** vary, that is, it costs some producers less than others to produce each loaf of bread. If any producer sells at a price that is less than their unit cost they will incur a loss; so the minimum price at which each producer is willing to sell is their unit cost. Table 3.2 gives the minimum price of each producer in our model.

Unit cost
The cost of producing one unit of that good.

TABLE 3.2 Producers' minimum prices

Producer	Minimum price
ABC	45p
Bakelite	49p
Crusty	56p
DeliLoaf	60p
Easybread	64p

Similarly, consumers differ both in how much they have to spend and how much they like bread, so they will have different *maximum* prices that they are willing to pay for a loaf of bread. If a loaf costs more than their maximum price they will use their money to buy something else. Such maximum prices show the value each consumer puts on a loaf of bread. Table 3.3 gives the maximum price each consumer is willing to pay in our model.

TABLE 3.3 Consumers' maximum prices

Consumer	Maximum price
Alex	70p
Brian	64p
Craig	58p
Damien	53p
Edward	49p

We now make another simplification and assume that each producer only sells at most one loaf and each consumer buys at most one loaf. Again this simplification should make the model easier to understand while retaining the main features of the process under investigation.

Producers make a surplus (a profit) from the difference between the price at which they sell their loaf and the unit cost of the loaf:

> Profit   =   Price – Unit cost   = **Producer's surplus**

Similarly, each consumer wants to buy their loaf at a low price to save money that could then be spent on other goods. The money that each consumer 'saves' is the difference between the price actually paid for the loaf and the maximum price that the consumer would have been willing to pay for it:

> 'Saving' = Maximum price – Price = **Consumer's surplus**

Both producers and consumers are interested in making their surpluses, profits and savings respectively, as large as possible.

4.1 Stage 1: No market

In order to understand what markets do to prices, it is useful to start by assuming that there is no market and instead a benevolent authority decides who will sell to whom. The authority does this by matching up all producers and consumers and fixing the price at which each pair deals, so that the producer sells at a profit and the consumer makes some 'saving' over the maximum price they would have been prepared to pay. In other words, all producers and consumers receive some surplus.

Producer's surplus
The difference between the price at which a producer sells a good and its unit cost of production.

Consumer's surplus
The difference between the maximum price the consumer would pay for a good and the actual price at which it is bought.

The outcome is represented in Table 3.4, in which each row represents a deal. The first row reports on Deal number 1. In this deal, the producer, ABC, sells a loaf to the consumer, Edward, for 47p (the price of the deal). We chose 47p because it is half-way between the minimum the producer would sell at, its unit cost (45p), and the maximum price the consumer would pay (49p), but we could have chosen any figure between 49p and 45p.

The producer's surplus (profit for ABC) is:

$$\text{Price of the deal} - \text{Unit cost} = 47p - 45p = 2p$$

The consumer's surplus (Edward's saving) is:

$$\text{Maximum price} - \text{Price of the deal} = 49p - 47p = 2p$$

The second row of Table 3.4 gives the same information for the deal between the producer Bakelite and the consumer Damien, who trade at 51p (column 6). The producer's surplus is calculated by subtracting its unit cost (column 3) from the price (column 6) and the consumer's surplus by subtracting the price (column 6) from the maximum price he would have been prepared to pay (column 5).

TABLE 3.4   Outcome of transactions under a benevolent authority

Deal number	Producer	Unit cost	Consumer	Max price	Price of the deal	Producer surplus (profit)	Consumer surplus (saving)
(1)	(2)	(3)	(4)	(5)	(6)	(7)	(8)
1	ABC	45p	Edward	49p	47p	2p	2p
2	Bakelite	49p	Damien	53p	51p	2p	2p
3	Crusty	56p	Craig	58p	57p		
4	DeliLoaf	60p	Brian	64p	62p		
5	Easybread	64p	Alex	70p	67p		
Total							

ACTIVITY 3.3

Calculate the remaining producers and consumers in a similar way and fill in the rest of columns 7 and 8 of the table. Then fill in the total producers' and consumers' surplus. (Answers are given at the end of the chapter.)

COMMENT

You should find that the outcome has the following characteristics:

- every producer and every consumer has made a deal with a positive surplus; nobody is excluded

- the deals are made at different prices ranging from 47p to 67p (column 6)

- the total surplus is 20p, which is found by adding the sum of total profit, 10p, from column 7, to total consumers' 'savings', also 10p, from column 8.

4.2 Stage 2: Introducing the market

Now, let's consider what happens if we start to introduce a market by letting buyers and sellers choose with whom to trade and at what price.

Agents could choose to trade with the same partner with whom they traded before under the benevolent authority (Stage 1 of the model). However, this is not very likely. ABC, the most efficient producer with the lowest unit costs (45p), knows that it has received the lowest price (47p) among all producers and that it can do a lot better. It will look for another consumer who is willing to pay more, such as Brian or Alex, whose maximum prices (64p and 70p respectively) are higher than Edward's (49p). Although it received a higher price than ABC, Bakelite also feels it could do better.

Similar considerations apply to consumers. Alex and Brian, who are paying high prices to inefficient producers, would do better by buying from producers who would accept lower prices. Would you choose to buy a product from an expensive store, when you can find exactly the same product cheaper somewhere else?

The following day, therefore, Alex trades with Bakelite and Brian trades with ABC at prices they can agree on, somewhere between the minimum the producers will accept and the maximum the consumers are willing to pay. Alex and Bakelite trade at, say, 59p, the average of their previous prices, while Brian and ABC trade at 54p. If Craig and Crusty stick to trading together, what will happen to DeliLoaf, Easybread, Edward and Damien, who were the trading partners of the four agents (Alex, Brian, ABC and Bakelite) that now trade together? We know that DeliLoaf is very inefficient – its unit costs, 60p, are among the highest. So DeliLoaf cannot trade profitably with Damien or Edward, both of whom have a maximum price (53p and 49p respectively) that is lower than DeliLoaf's unit costs. The same applies to Easybread, whose unit costs, 64p, are even higher than DeliLoaf's.

DeliLoaf and Easybread are also excluded from the market because they cannot sell at a profit. Similarly Damien and Edward don't buy bread and spend their money elsewhere.

Table 3.5 summarizes the outcome of this second stage.

TABLE 3.5   Outcome of transactions: beginnings of a market

Deal number	Producer	Unit cost	Consumer	Max price	Price of the deal	Producer surplus (profit)	Consumer surplus (saving)
(1)	(2)	(3)	(4)	(5)	(6)	(7)	(8)
1	ABC	45p	Brian	64p	59p		
2	Bakelite	49p	Alex	70p	54p		
3	Crusty	56p	Craig	58p	57p		
Total							

ACTIVITY 3.4

Complete Columns 7 and 8 of Table 3.5.

(Answers are given at end of this chapter.)

COMMENT

The completed table shows the following:

- Only three deals have occurred and four agents have been left out of the market.

- The range of prices has reduced considerably; they now vary from 54p to 59p, with a range of only 5p, while before they varied from 47p to 67p, a range of 20p. This is because the exclusion of DeliLoaf and Easybread, who needed high prices to be profitable, and Damien and Edward, who needed low prices to be willing to buy, has reduced the range of possible prices.

- From the last row of the table we can see that the total surplus is substantially larger now than before (20p+22p=42p rather than 20p) despite only three deals having been carried out instead of five. This is a result of the range of prices being reduced and both inefficient producers and consumers who value the good less than others being excluded from trading.

4.3 Stage 3: Equilibrium prices

However, some agents feel there is still scope for improvement. Brian and Craig, who have paid 59p and 57p respectively, would prefer to buy bread at 54p, which is the price that Alex paid. On the other hand, Bakelite and Crusty, who sold at 54p and 57p would make more profit charging 59p, which is what ABC sold at. *While prices are different, agents know there is always scope for improvement.* This is competition in the market. Producers and consumers keep looking for new trading partners and better prices until all trades occur at one single price.

So, prices tend to become more and more equal until they converge on a single price. When there is a single price, the market is in equilibrium because no agent has any incentive to change what they are doing. Table 3.6 shows the results when everyone trades at the same equilibrium price.

TABLE 3.6   Outcome of transactions with an equilibrium prices

Deal number	Producer	Unit cost	Consumer	Max price	Price of the deal	Producer surplus (profit)	Consumer surplus (saving)
(1)	(2)	(3)	(4)	(5)	(6)	(7)	(8)
1	ABC	45p	Brian	64p	57p	12p	7p
2	Bakelite	49p	Alex	70p	57p	8p	13p
3	Crusty	56p	Craig	58p	57p	1p	1p
Total						21p	21p

C O M M E N T

The completed table shows the following:

- The total surplus in the market is the same as in the previous case. The total surplus has not changed because the same six agents are trading, although at different prices. No further increases have resulted from inefficient producers or consumers who do not value bread enough being excluded from the market. This is a limitation caused by the simplicity of this model. With more agents and more stages, further increases in the total surplus would have been possible.

- The process of convergence towards the equilibrium price happened through the interaction of agents looking to increase their individual surplus. It is as though the market was an invisible hand that guided these self-interested agents to maximize the total surplus available.

This is a model for which there is some empirical support. In experimental situations with artificial markets, prices do tend to converge rather quickly to a single equilibrium value. In the economy we find that in many markets where goods are homogeneous (that is, there are no significant differences in quality or appearance) the prices charged by sellers are so close that it is hardly worth shopping around; the market does it for you.

4.4 A market with multiple sales

This is as far as we can get with this model in this form. However, we can learn some more if we relax the assumption that each firm can only sell one loaf to one consumer. This is a usual step in building models; having learned what we can from a particularly simple one, we see what happens if we complicate the model just a little. By allowing firms to sell more than one loaf, we are introducing a more realistic form of competition into the model.

If firms can sell more than one loaf and can sell to more than one consumer, the most efficient firm, ABC, will be able to undercut the prices offered by all other firms. In order to do this ABC must charge a price at which all other firms would make a loss; this price is at most 48p, since at 49p Bakelite can break even. Provided the price is not higher than their maximum price, all consumers will buy a loaf; at a price of 49p or less, this would include Damien and Edward who had previously dropped out of the market. Let's suppose ABC chooses to set the price at 48p to make as much profit as it can while excluding all its competitors.

TABLE 3.7   Results of market transactions with multiple sales

Deal number	Producer	Unit cost	Consumer	Max price	Price of the deal	Producer surplus (profit)	Consumer surplus (saving)
(1)	(2)	(3)	(4)	(5)	(6)	(7)	(8)
1	ABC	45p	Alex	70p	48p		
2	ABC	45p	Brian	64p	48p		
3	ABC	45p	Craig	58p	48p		
4	ABC	45p	Damien	53p	48p		
5	ABC	45p	Edward	49p	48p		
Total							

ACTIVITY 3.5

Complete Columns 7 and 8 of Table 3.7.

(Answers are given at end of this chapter.)

COMMENT

The completed table shows the following:

- The equilibrium price has fallen drastically (from 57p to 48p) because of competition between firms. As a result of the competitive process only the most efficient firm is producing and it has to sell at a fairly low price in order for other firms not to steal its customers. The new equilibrium price is above the unit cost of the most efficient firm but below that of any less efficient firm.

- No other firms are included in the market: ABC sells all 5 loaves that are traded.

- All consumers are included now that the price is lower – however, if there were consumers that had a maximum price below 45p they would be still excluded, even if ABC dropped the price as low as it could, given that its unit cost is 45p.

- The number of loaves ABC can sell depends on how many consumers are willing to pay this price. This means that consumers govern how many loaves are produced. This is an aspect of what is called consumer sovereignty.

- As a result of competition between firms, the total surplus has risen considerably (from 42p to 69p). The surplus mainly goes to consumers because any firm has to keep its price low to exclude competitors.

In this model we had just one producer who was more efficient than all the rest; this producer was therefore a monopolist, that is, the only seller in the market. But this is not a necessary feature. If we extended the model further and had more producers, each of whom could sell as many loaves as they liked, the most efficient producers could undercut all the less efficient producers. Competition between them would drive the price down to just above the unit costs of the most efficient producers. This would whittle the producers' surplus away and boost the consumers' surplus. So where there is competition between producers, consumers make all the gains.

SUMMARY

The model shows that when self-interested producers and consumers are free to choose their trading partner, producers seek consumers who are willing to pay high prices and consumers seek producers who are willing to accept low prices. We can make some general points about such a market process.

- Consumers who are not willing to pay much for the good, either because they have low incomes or do not like the good much, and inefficient producers who cannot sell at a low price are excluded

- The range of prices at which deals take place tends to become narrower over time until prices converge towards a single equilibrium price.

- Such convergence happens as a consequence of economic agents pursuing their own interests; no external authority co-ordinates the market. This is an example of Smith's 'invisible hand' in action; it requires no benevolence or concern for others on the part of economic agents to achieve a co-ordinated outcome.

- As prices converge towards the equilibrium price, the total surplus increases as inefficient producers and consumers who are not willing to pay as much for the good are excluded from the market.

- Competition between producers favours consumers since they gain the benefits of being able to buy from the most efficient producers. Consumers decide what is produced and in what quantity through their actions in the market; how much of the good is produced depends on how much consumers value it. This is an aspect of what's been called 'consumer sovereignty'.

- Not all consumers are equally 'sovereign' in the market: their influence depends on how much money they have to spend.

5 EXTERNALITIES AND THE 'INVISIBLE ELBOW'

The neoclassical model of the market outlined in Section 4 seems to provide a strong rationale for leaving the allocation of resources to markets. The model shows that competition ensures that markets are efficient so that resources are used in the way that best reflects consumers' values. So we can say that, on the one hand, markets are social structures in which the pressure of competition constrains the behaviour of economic agents. On the other hand, the model emphasizes the scope for agency that consumers have in the market, because of the freedom and sovereignty that the market process gives them.

So if we as consumers care about the environment, the market should listen to us. If the environment is not protected in a market economy, perhaps it is because consumers do not value it enough or because the ones who do value it have too little money to spend – after all, environmentally friendly goods are sold in the market. Is the problem simply that we do not value the environment sufficiently – we don't put our money where our mouth is – or is there something missing in this 'invisible hand' model of how markets work that matters when we use it for looking at the environment? Are natural resources in some way different from the type of commodities that we have been using so far to illustrate how markets work?

5.1 Externalities

As we noted earlier, environmental damage is usually an unintended consequence of actions taken for quite different reasons. This is because the effects of environmental damage are typically experienced by people other than those who cause it. In a market economy, decisions about the use of resources are left to individual economic agents, who will, in general, decide what to do on the basis of the **private costs and benefits** to themselves, rather than by considering the wider effects of their actions on society as a whole – the **social costs and benefits**. Private costs have to be paid for; a firm has to pay its labour force, buy raw materials, invest in machinery, etc. However, a decision to produce something may also cause social costs, costs for others, for example, through damaging the environment. As these are costs that the decision makers do not have to pay, they are unlikely to take them into account when deciding what to do.

"It may be industrial effluent to you lad—but it's a new Bentley and a heated swimming pool to me."

The 'responsibility' for environmental degradation does not only lie with producers. Consumers who buy from them will also pay less than the full cost of the products they consume. When we decide to buy food produced using pesticides because it is cheaper than organic food, we pay a price that reflects only the private costs of producing it, and we let society as a whole foot the bill for the difference between the social and the private costs. When private and social costs diverge, the market allows environmental damage to be caused as the unintended consequences of the exercise of consumer choice and the pursuit of profit by producers. In such cases, we say that there is an **externality**, because some of the cost is external to the decision makers.

Externalities can be positive or negative. The flowers we grow in our gardens for our own enjoyment may also give pleasure to our neighbours; this is a positive externality. Most environmental problems, however, arise from negative externalities, where producers or consumers do not bear the full social costs of their own decisions. This is most obvious when waste is

Private costs and benefits
The private costs and benefits of a market transaction are those costs and benefits incurred by the buyers and sellers involved in the transaction.

Social costs and benefits
The social costs and benefits of a market transaction include, in addition to private costs and benefits, those costs and benefits incurred by other agents not involved in the transaction.

Externality
Externalities occur when private costs and benefits differ from social costs and benefits. In such cases, economic agents do not pay the full costs or enjoy the full benefits of their action.

dumped elsewhere, as in the acid rain produced by the industry of one country falling on another. But it is also true when those who cause the problem are not the only people who experience it, as in the cases of fish stocks being depleted or smoke polluting the atmosphere. In these cases the environmental damage is a cost to everyone, but if only the cost to themselves is taken into account by decision makers, this will be much less than the full social cost.

FIGURE 3.4   Forest killed by acid rain, Poland

An economic system that depends on the market to co-ordinate individual decisions is prone to externalities and the environmental problems these produce. We can examine how these are caused and some of the remedies proposed, by looking at the three different types of environmental problems we mentioned in the introduction to this chapter.

5.1.1 Exhaustible resources

Many of the world's natural resources, such as forests and fish stocks, can become exhausted if not used judiciously. If anyone can make use of them there is always a tendency for them to be overused. The problem here is that the full costs of overfishing, for example, are not borne by the individuals who do it. Overfishing causes costs for others; these are negative externalities. Individuals who catch fish gain income from selling it. However, if this catch reduces subsequent fishing opportunities, this imposes costs on everyone who might fish in the future. These costs will get passed on to the future customers who will have to pay higher prices. In this case the individuals who fish bear only a part of the total social costs of their fishing. Further, an environmentally conscious individual reducing his or her catch wouldn't help. Unless everyone reduces their catch, any individual who reduced his or her catch will lose income from having less fish to sell, but still suffer the consequences of everyone else's overfishing. Without any other form of co-ordination, market forces give each individual a powerful incentive to catch as many fish as possible.

One solution that has been suggested by some economists in such a case is to make sure exhaustible resources are privately owned. If the seas were privately owned and their owners charged others for fishing in them, the owners would look after the fish stocks because they would be concerned about losing fishing revenues in the future; if the fish stocks were running out, they would not be able to charge so much for fishing. Overfishing would be a cost to the owners. In other words, what are currently the external costs of fishing would become private costs to the owners. To cover these costs, the owners would charge a fee for fishing that reflected the full social cost; there would no longer be any externalities. So it could be argued that in the case of exhaustible resources the problem of externalities is caused by the fact that the market is missing. Markets need property rights in order to work; if nobody owns a resource, the incentives of the market are missing. The solution to such externalities and the environmental problems they cause is to introduce the market by granting property rights over all exhaustible resources.

The problem, however, with this solution is that it is not clear that a private owner would necessarily take into account all social costs in the way you or I would want. Think of a forest, for example, although it might be in the interest of private owners to ensure their future income and restrict logging by charging for it, there is no guarantee that they will choose to do so in such a way that will preserve or replenish the forest. It might turn out to be in their interest to flatten it and develop housing on it. All private ownership does is privatize the costs of overuse, but some other externalities, such as those due to the effects on the level of carbon dioxide from cutting down the forests, may still arise. Further, the forest owners may have different priorities than you or I, and if the sums don't work out for them in favour of preserving the forest, the market will not save it.

FIGURE 3.5
Surui Indian children watch a logging road being cut through their reservation in the Amazon

An alternative solution would be to put it into social ownership, with society managing the resource and charging for or controlling its use in other ways. The buying and selling of fishing quotas allocated by the European Union is an example of this. National or supra-national control is not the only form social ownership can take; traditionally, many societies managed to preserve their natural resources through social norms controlling their use. However, the encroachment of the market on people's lives frequently breaks down such traditional norms.

5.1.2 Public goods

It is not always possible to allocate property rights in a common resource. Certain common resources, such as clean air, are known as **public goods**. For such goods, it is not possible to exclude others from their consumption. For example, we all breathe the same air. This means that even if people value it the market cannot provide clean air. If someone wanted to pay to have cleaner air for herself, she could only do this by paying for everyone to have cleaner air. She would not be able to recoup any of her expenses because others, known as 'free riders', could not be prevented from using the cleaner air that she had paid for. If everyone benefits, whether or not they pay, why should anyone pay?

Public goods: These are goods (such as air) for which it is impossible to exclude others from consumption, and the consumption of which does not reduce the total amount available.

So in the case of public goods, the externalities that arise from their being held in common cannot be avoided by establishing private property rights. Even if we wanted to, we could not create private ownership of a public good such as the air; it would be meaningless since an owner could not stop everyone else using it. In this case the only solution would be social ownership. In a market economy this would mean a payment to people who created or improved public goods and a charge, or tax, on those who despoiled them. This is the idea behind 'green taxes' which make polluters pay the costs of the damage they cause. This corrects, or at least reduces, the externality.

5.1.3 Future generations

The third type of environmental problem referred to in the introduction involved the interests of future generations being hurt by the actions of people alive today. In this case, the problem is that the social costs that impact only in the future may be nobody's current private costs; today's activities can cause big negative externalities for future generations. Consumers influence the outcome of markets only through the money they have to spend. The interests of future generations are ignored by the market because they have no purchasing power. There may be some ways in which the interests of future generations are represented indirectly, for example by current parents, but even with the best of intentions they are likely to put less value on the future than their children would. To anyone alive today, the quality of air we breathe today will matter at least as much if not more than the quality of the air in the year 2100, but to children born in 2099 only the latter will matter.

Again there appears to be very limited market solutions to this problem. Various political solutions have been suggested including appointing guardians to look after the interest of future generations. But such guardians can only work by going against the market; the market in itself cannot properly look after the interests of people not yet born.

5.2 The 'invisible hand' and the 'invisible elbow'

As we saw in Section 2, one of the strengths of the market is that it co-ordinates the decisions of individual consumers and producers, without any of them needing to take account of what others are doing. Each simply had to know the prices at which he could buy and sell goods in order to decide what to do. Further, the outcome brought general prosperity, even though each participant looked only to his own interest. However, in this section we have seen how, in the context of externalities, this same characteristic, that people do not need to take account of what others are doing, is the market's weakness. People need have no idea of the environmental damage their economic decisions may be causing. Consumers, even if they care about the environment, are not informed by the market about the environmental impact of the products they buy. Nor, indeed, are producers informed about costs they impose on others, unless they are required to pay for them. So the environmental impact of market transactions is typically inadvertent.

This happens because, in markets, agents make their decisions solely on the basis of prices. The failure of markets to care for the environment suggests that, if we are concerned with preserving the environment, the information summarized in the price of goods is incomplete. The price mechanism that we have explored in our model is good at maximizing the total monetary surplus in a market, but it fails to deal with other issues that might be important, such as environmental degradation or ethical issues. When we buy a good because it is cheaper we don't know whether the only reason it is cheaper is, for example, because it has been produced by a more polluting technology or by using child labour.

The environmentalist Michael Jacobs talks about this phenomenon as the 'invisible elbow' of market forces, saying that a counterpart to 'the "invisible hand" which Adam Smith argued brought general prosperity... can equally be an "invisible elbow" which brings general ruin. ... often elbows are not used deliberately at all; they knock things over inadvertently' (Jacobs, 1991, p.25).

SUMMARY

- Environmental problems are often caused by externalities that occur when agents do not have to pay all the costs of their actions.

- Where there are externalities, private and social costs differ. Where social costs are greater than private costs, agents may carry out actions that they would not have carried out if they had to pay all the cost of their actions.

- Externalities lie behind the environmental problems that occur when exhaustible resources are depleted, when public goods are spoiled and when future generations have to pay the cost of current actions.

- Policies to overcome the problems caused by such externalities include putting exhaustible resources in private ownership and making agents pay the full costs of their actions through imposing green taxes.

- A market economy is inherently prone to externalities because economic agents make their decisions on the basis of price alone and do not necessarily know or care about external costs. In a market economy, externalities function like an 'invisible elbow' that inadvertently knocks over those things that are not accounted for by the 'invisible hand'.

6 CONTROLLING THE 'INVISIBLE ELBOW'

We have just seen that market economies are prone to externalities, because the price mechanism does not provide agents with all the information about the wider consequences of their actions, and people are not encouraged to consider interests other than their own. Moreover, even if people were informed and environmentally concerned, market forces may leave them no room for manoeuvre. Competition forces producers to cut costs wherever they can to survive – this will include off-loading costs through externalities wherever possible, especially if their competitors are already doing so.

So what can be done to have the benefits of the 'invisible hand' co-ordinating the market but keep the 'invisible elbow' under control? Two types of market solutions were proposed in the previous section: extending private ownership by assigning property rights, and green taxes and subsidies to bring private costs in line with social costs. However, these market solutions pose some problems that arise from distributional issues, usually from the fact that existing resources are not equally distributed among economic agents.

The solution based on assigning property rights immediately begs the question to whom should such rights be assigned? In practice, in past 'privatizations' of this kind, such as the enclosure movement in England, those who were better off were allocated the bigger share of the previously common land. But even if property rights are equally divided among the population with a claim on a resource, the outcome in the long run is still likely to favour the rich. This is for two reasons. First, the free use of resources held in common, such as common land, is likely to have made more difference to the living standards of the poor than to those of the rich. So even if the poor gain as much as the rich from privatization, they lose more in comparison with the past. Second, markets have a tendency to concentrate resources. Private property can be sold for money, and money is more likely to be needed urgently by the poor than by the rich. So for one reason or another, a bad harvest perhaps, poor people are more likely to end up reducing their holdings, and rich people are more likely to be able to expand theirs by buying other's shares.

Externalities also have distributional implications because they are costs imposed by one agent on others. There won't be only one way to correct that externality and each way will have specific distributional effects. In particular, externalities can be corrected by providing either carrots or sticks. For example, the government could either subsidize farmers using an environmentally friendly way of controlling pests or tax those who use environmentally dangerous pesticides. A green subsidy is just like a negative green tax; it too can be used to correct a difference between social costs and private costs, to encourage environmentally friendly actions where private costs are too high.

6.1 Power in the market

A significant problem with making the market work better is that it will reflect some people's wishes more than others; some consumers are more 'sovereign' than others.

As you saw in Section 2, when resources such as coffee become scarce, the price will rise and people who are prepared to pay more for their coffee will continue to drink it; those not prepared to pay as much will switch to other drinks. The total quantity of coffee produced will be determined by a myriad of such decisions about how much each individual is prepared to pay for a cup of coffee. If what you are prepared to pay also depends on your income, the influence of people with more income will be greater than that of poorer people in determining, for example, how much coffee is produced, how much oil is extracted, how much pollution is allowed.

This problem of unequal power is a feature of the way markets work. Markets give power to people in accordance with the money they have to spend. This is because the only way to make needs and wishes felt through the market is to be prepared to pay for them, in order to turn those wishes into 'effective demand' or spending power. How much one's wishes can be put in the form of effective demand will depend on how much money one has to spend rather than the importance of those wishes in any objective sense. A peasant village that is unable to raise the few hundred dollars needed to have a water pump in their village will have a much less effective claim on their own local water supply than consumers in the west who are spending thousands of dollars on buying out-of-season vegetables that depend on water from the same source.

Richer people may be able to avoid the effects of environmental degradation more easily than poorer people, by paying more for their fish, by buying bottled water or by buying houses in lower risk environments. This means that they may have less stake in avoiding environmental degradation than poorer people. But the rich have more power in the market place and so the market solution will take more account of their views. The answer that the market comes up with about the 'right' amount of environmental degradation may not be one with which the poor agree. It is only 'right' in the sense that the market balances the effective demands of rich and poor and this is a very unequal contest.

The people with the least effective demand are those that have no money at all. These include most children alive today and all generations not yet born. They have no way of turning their wishes into direct effective demand. Instead they have to rely on others doing it for them, but the fact that children are more likely to live in poverty than adults in all countries (except in a few Northern European welfare states) suggests that relying on other people does not often lead to equitable outcomes. This also means that concerns about the condition in which we are leaving the planet for future generations are unlikely to be addressed by a market solution.

6.2 The problems of valuing the environment

Green taxes and subsidies also pose the question of the level at which they should be set. Ideally they should be set at a level that makes the private costs of any activity equal to its social costs. But how can those costs be assessed? Where the costs are borne by profit-making firms there may be a way of measuring the profits lost as a result of a specific polluting activity. But what about the costs to the population more widely and to future generations?

One way to measure such costs is to ask people how much they would be prepared to pay not to have the pollution or, alternatively, how much they would need to be paid to put up with it. However, again there are distributional issues raised by this. Rich people might be able to pay more not to suffer from the effects of pollution and might need to be paid more to agree to put up with it than poorer people could or would. Does this mean that polluters should be taxed more highly for polluting areas in which rich people live? If this was the case then polluting firms would locate in poorer parts of the world. This relocation can also happen because richer countries have felt able to impose tougher environmental regulations on firms than poorer countries. This is because the revenues that such firms bring is needed more by poorer countries than richer ones. Not surprisingly, the worst polluting industries are located in the poorest parts of the world.

Finally there is the issue of how we measure the cost that environmental problems will impose on future generations. They cannot be asked how much they would pay not to have such problems, so we have to find an answer by imagining ourselves in their position. Another problem then arises of how to value what happens in future years compared with what happens today. Most people alive today would argue that the compensation needed to persuade them to accept pollution today would be more than that needed to accept pollution to be suffered in ten years' time, and much greater than for pollution to be suffered in one hundred years' time. But members of future generations will not think like this, since the effects of pollution suffered today are no problem to them.

6.3 Beyond the market

Finally some things that are lost through environmental degradation may be impossible to value. How can you put a value on the beauty of the countryside? It doesn't just mean the loss of a resource. You may never make use of the countryside, but you can still appreciate its existence and care that it continues not only for your own or your children's enjoyment but also for the community more widely. The neoclassical model that you examined in Section 2 worked on the assumption that all wants could be satisfied by the consumption of goods and services. If that was the case then we *could* put a value on them. But other wants and needs cannot be analysed in the same way as a desire for consumption goods.

Similarly, in the neoclassical model all resources are privately owned. The neoclassical solution is to make the world like their model and make sure all material resources are privately owned. We might have other reasons for not wanting to extend private ownership. We may put a positive value on living in a society in which the mountains and the seashore belong to us all, rather than one in which property rights are parcelled out.

Finally, the neoclassical model works on the assumption that everyone acts according to their self-interest and builds its picture of the economy on this basis. But perhaps in reality it is the other way around. Perhaps it is living in a market economy that makes people act in their own self-interest and lose any sense of responsibility for the effects of their actions on the environment. As social scientists, we need to recognize that people behave differently in

"We do our best here to build a better world for the next generation — of nuclear reactors, that is."

different sorts of society. If we lived in a more environmentally friendly society, one in which people cared more about each other and therefore about the environment, externalities might not be the problem that they are today.

SUMMARY

- All market solutions to environmental problems have distributional implications. They will hurt some people and favour others. In particular, assigning property rights may deprive poorer people of access to common resources that they depend on more than richer people. Further, markets tend to concentrate privately held resources thus increasing income inequality.

- Market solutions to environmental problems might also not be fair because people who are wealthier have a greater power in decisions that are taken 'by the market'. It is not the number of people affected, but the money that can be spent on something that matters.

- How to value the environment in order to set green taxes or subsidies is not a straightforward technical issue, it is open to much political debate, especially when the interests of future generations are involved.

- The market model assumes that people's desires to own and consume material things is more important than anything else, but it is possible that people value other things, such as the nature of the society in which they live.

- Instead of markets being the solution, they may be part of the problem. It may be living in a market economy that makes people not know, not care or not be able to do anything about the effects of their actions on the environment.

7 CONCLUSION

This chapter has given you a flavour of the debates about the effects of economic activity on environmental degradation, especially focusing on market economies. In doing so, we introduced a simplified model that focused on the price mechanism, as a way of understanding markets. We learnt about the power of the price mechanism, but also its limitations, especially as far as environmental degradation is concerned. We saw how the existence of externalities in markets can make the simplicity of the price mechanism dangerous for the environment. Market prices provide neither information nor the incentives needed for agents to make decisions that take the environment into consideration.

We briefly examined possible corrections to the market that could help limit environmental degradation, such as the introduction of property rights to combat the excessive exploitation of exhaustible resources and green taxes and subsidies. We also saw that distributional issues are not only about who gains and loses from such policies but also about the power that individuals have in the market; those who have more money will have more say in the outcomes that result. This will not always reflect the value that other, poorer people may put on the environment.

We also saw that the neoclassical approach assumes that people are concerned only about their own interests and that these interests can be reduced to the ownership and consumption of material goods. But people may care about other issues, such as the type of society in which they live and the natural environment that surrounds them. Further, the type of society in which people live may affect whether and how people care about the environment.

REFERENCES

Maddison, A. (1991) *Dynamic Forces in Capitalist Development: A Long-run Comparative View,* Oxford, Oxford University Press.

Maddison, A. (1995) *Monitoring the World Economy, 1820-1992,* Paris, Development Centre Study of the OECD.

Jacobs, M. (1991) *The Green Economy,* London, Pluto Press.

Smith, A. (1776) *An Inquiry into the Nature and Causes of the Wealth of Nations* 1971 edn, eds Campbell, R.H. and Skinner, A.S., Oxford, Clarendon Press.

FURTHER READING

Bowers, J. (1997) *Sustainability and Economics: An Alternative Text,* London, Longman – a critique of neoclassical environmental economics for students of economics. The author is both an economist and an environmental campaigner.

Andre Gorz (1994) *Capitalism, Socialism, Ecology,* London, Verso – a socialist view on the relationship between politics, economics and the environment.

Michael Jacobs (1991) *The Green Economy,* London, Pluto Press – a very clear account of a whole range of economic positions on the environment, from a perspective critical of the neoclassical orthodoxy.

David Pearce (1993) *Economic Values and the Natural World,* London, Earthscan Publications – a clear but occasionally slightly technical account of the neoclassical position.

Peter Saunders (1995) *Capitalism: A Social Audit,* Buckingham, Open University Press – an enthusiastic view of how the neoclassical model can make capitalism and environmentalism work together.

Schumacher, F. (1973) *Small is Beautiful: Economics as if People Really Mattered,* London, Abacus – a classic and pioneering work of environmental thought written for the general reader.

ANSWER TO ACTIVITY 3.3

The completed table should look like this:

Deal number	Producer	Unit cost	Consumer	Max price	Price of the deal	Producer surplus (profit)	Consumer surplus (saving)
(1)	(2)	(3)	(4)	(5)	(6)	(7)	(8)
1	ABC	45p	Edward	49p	47p	2p	2p
2	Bakelite	49p	Damien	53p	51p	2p	2p
3	Crusty	56p	Craig	58p	57p	1p	1p
4	DeliLoaf	60p	Brian	64p	62p	2p	2p
5	Easybread	64p	Alex	70p	67p	3p	3p
Total						10p	10p

ANSWER TO ACTIVITY 3.4

The completed table should look like this:

Deal number	Producer	Unit cost	Consumer	Max price	Price of the deal	Producer surplus (profit)	Consumer surplus (saving)
(1)	(2)	(3)	(4)	(5)	(6)	(7)	(8)
1	ABC	45p	Brian	64p	59p	14p	5p
2	Bakelite	49p	Alex	70p	54p	5p	16p
3	Crusty	56p	Craig	58p	57p	1p	1p
Total						20p	22p

ANSWER TO ACTIVITY 3.5

The completed table should look like this:

Deal number	Producer	Unit cost	Consumer	Max price	Price of the deal	Producer surplus (profit)	Consumer surplus (saving)
(1)	(2)	(3)	(4)	(5)	(6)	(7)	(8)
1	ABC	45p	Alex	70p	48p	3p	22p
2	ABC	45p	Brian	64p	48p	3p	16p
3	ABC	45p	Craig	58p	48p	3p	10p
4	ABC	45p	Damien	53p	48p	3p	5p
5	ABC	45p	Edward	49p	48p	3p	1p
Total						15p	54p

Living with risk: the unnatural geography of environmental crises

Steve Hinchliffe

chapter 4

Contents

1	**Introduction**	**118**
2	**The unnatural geography of natural hazards**	**119**
	2.1 Who or what gets the blame for natural hazards?	121
	2.2 Who benefits from conventional explanations of natural hazards?	127
	2.3 Let them eat bananas – the uneven geographies of risk	128
3	**Living risky lives – eating outer nature**	**136**
	3.1 Do cows make you mad?	137
	3.2 What the experts said	141
	3.3 Rationalities and cultures of risk	144
4	**Conclusion**	**151**
	References	**152**
	Further reading	**153**

1   INTRODUCTION

Throughout this book you have repeatedly been asked to question the idea that nature and society exist as separate categories. So, in Chapter 1, human identities and childhood development were shown to be the results of complex interactions between what we have been used to calling social and natural matters. The implication was that if we fail to recognize the importance of these interactions we end up with a limited understanding of what it can mean to be human. Likewise, you read in Chapter 2 that a person's health is a product of a mixture of social conditions, bodily matters and environmental quality. Failing to take account of one or more of these may well reduce the effectiveness with which we can deal with ill health. Finally, in Chapter 3 you read that our lives are bound up with market practices. Arguably, there is no place on the planet that isn't touched in some way by markets. If we fail to take account of the ways in which markets work then we will miss an awful lot of the current means by which nature and society are being mixed together and churned up on a daily basis.

After reading the previous chapters you may be thinking that nature and society are now so thoroughly mixed together that it makes little sense to use the terms at all. In all of the examples it is very difficult to identify where society stops and nature starts, and vice versa. One things is for sure, the diagram used in the book Introduction to represent purified notions of the social and the natural depicts a mode of understanding that is of very little use in helping us to understand the issues that have been raised in this book. You might like to experiment with alternative diagrams as you read on. In any case, we will come back to the diagram in the Afterword to this book.

Now, given this mixed up state of affairs, we can ask a number of questions. These are the central questions for this chapter. You should write them down and aim to answer them as you work through the chapter:

1   If society and nature are no more than two sides of the same coin, why do we often talk as if they are separate matters?

2   What do we gain and what do we lose by holding nature and society apart like this in our thoughts?

3   Can we carry on for much longer thinking that society and nature are essentially amenable to separation?

These may seem to be rather abstract questions. This is not something that is necessarily foreign to social science. Nevertheless, social scientists do often seek to develop their ideas with reference to specific issues. They look to particular instances and for evidence. These may help to support their ideas or may end up challenging them. Either way, social science is often a matter of being involved in the world, asking questions of it and allowing it to ask questions of you. To this end, we can develop some answers to the three questions by focusing upon particular themes and issues. The theme for this chapter is environmental **risk**. The issues are natural hazards and food scares.

We start, in Section 2, by looking at natural hazards, concentrating in particular on extreme weather events. With an eye on question 1 (above), I will ask just how natural are natural hazards and why is it that we describe them as natural in the first place? We shall then compare two risk events, one that was described as a largely social affair and one that was attributed to nature. The comparison will help to offer some answers to question 2. In Section 3 the focus shifts to food production and consumption. The risks associated with food manage to bring society and inner and outer natures together in ways that are often arresting. We shall look in particular at the 'mad cow' or BSE (Bovine Spongiform Encephalopathy) crisis that developed in Britain in the 1980s and 1990s. The aim will be to use this case to develop some further thoughts on question 2 and to open up answers to question 3.

In sum, the aim of this chapter is to investigate environmental risk by highlighting the ways in which the two poles of nature and society become entangled as we look more closely at threats and hazards. In addition, the argument will be made that part of our current predicament with regard to environmental risks is that we tend to view the world as made up of bits of society and bits of nature. Once we start to collapse these distinctions we may be in a better position to live more effectively with risk.

Risk
Exposure to dangers, adverse conditions and threats. To take a risk is to know that an action may prove costly. The magnitude of the risks may be relatively well known (in the form of a probability), or they may be largely unpredictable.

2   THE UNNATURAL GEOGRAPHY OF NATURAL HAZARDS

The one thing that you can always rely on in Britain is the unreliability of the weather. In 1998, the British climate seemed to have been unusually unreliable. And the damage was immense (particularly for the people who lived in areas of storm damage or flooding). At the start of the year, 'freak' windstorms tore off roofs in Selsey Bill. At the end of the year, storm-driven waves battered the coastline to such an extent that parts of Beachy Head, near Eastbourne, crumbled into the sea. The weather-beaten British Isles seemed to be caving in, physically, and in the case of the white,

FIGURE 4.1   A weather-beaten coastal town – Tynemouth, north-east England

chalk cliffs of south-east England, symbolically. Easter, 1998, saw large parts of England and Wales under water. Five people died as a result of the floods. Over 4,000 properties were flooded. In autumn, the floods returned. People started to look for someone or something to blame. People wanted to know the cause of all this damage and disruption to the established order. In the distant past, accidents were blamed on the gods, a God or some other supernatural entity. Today we tend to look for new scapegoats or 'non-caused causes' (see Box 4.1). In Section 2.1, we shall look at who or what gets the blame for such events. Sections 2.2 and 2.3 then discuss who or what benefits from the ways in which we explain such hazards and risks.

BOX 4.1	**Acts of God to acts of El Niño – a cause without a cause, a new scapegoat?**

El Niño is a name used to describe the warm oceanic and atmospheric conditions that can occur along the western coast of Ecuador and Peru. The term initially referred to the annual shift in ocean currents that brings warm weather around the end of December (El Niño means 'baby' in Spanish and refers to the events surrounding the nativity in the Christian calendar). El Niño now more generally refers to an unusually intense occurrence of this annual shift which brings even warmer atmospheric and oceanic conditions. These unusual events occur every three to seven years.

El Niño has been a topic of conversation in Peru, Ecuador and Chile for centuries, as it tends to disrupt the availability of fish in the region. Now meteorologists argue that the change in air and ocean temperatures can not only disrupt the weather and economy locally, its can also have effects across the entire Pacific region and even further afield.

El Niño became the prime suspect for many of the word's ills in 1998. From strange weather to economic instability, almost everything was being linked to the shift in ocean currents. The media exposure given to El Niño was so great in the United States that there was a report that a man named Al Nino, who lived in Texas, was receiving telephone calls lambasting him for all the havoc he was causing.

Without underestimating the physical power of El Niño, it is easy to see it as a convenient scapegoat. El Niño was thought to be a natural process, for which nothing else was to blame. The convenience is that this type of non-caused cause gets everyone else off the hook (except poor Al Nino). So-called 'natural' phenomena like El Niño are useful because they provide the means for downplaying human complicity in world events.

Unfortunately, El Niño may soon lose its status as a non-caused cause. The possible causes of El Niño are themselves now under scrutiny. Some meteorologists are arguing that human-induced climate changes are contributing to the increased frequency and intensity of the baby. It may no longer be so easy to deny human complicity in world events. Or we may simply need another scapegoat.

2.1 Who or what gets the blame for natural hazards?

The clue to answering this question is in the name – natural hazards. We can take an example to see how this blame game pans out. The extract in the following Activity is an attempt to pin the blame on to something. It was written by employees of the Environment Agency, an organization responsible for, amongst other things, flood defences and the issuing of flood warnings in England and Wales. It might be useful to note that, after the Easter floods in England and Wales in 1998, a finger of suspicion was being pointed at the Agency for certain alleged failures of responsibility. The details of the account are not important. What is important is the attempt that is being made to identify the causes for the flooding.

ACTIVITY 4.1

As you read the extract in Reading 4.1, note down who or what is being blamed for the floods. Who is being exonerated?

Preliminary report on the Easter floods, Environment Agency, April 1998

So far, April 1998 is the wettest April for 100 years and is likely to be the wettest since records began. Most rain fell between 8 and 19 April. During Wednesday 8 April and Thursday 9 April an area of unstable air met an area of rising air associated with a weather front. Heavy thundery showers occurred in the unstable air along the front. The combination of these two processes led to the very high rainfall totals observed over a short period of time [...]. The Met Office forecast for Easter – 'cold with rain, heavy at times' – grossly underestimated the actual rainfall.

and

Exceptionally heavy rain fell on parts of Wales and Central England over Easter, causing widespread flooding. Initial estimates indicate over 4,200 properties were flooded from surface water run-off or rivers overtopping banks or flood defences and spilling into the flood plain. Flood defences in many of the hardest hit areas, such as Northampton and Banbury, were not designed for floods of the magnitude seen over Easter, which might be expected to occur perhaps once in every 100 to 150 years. Tragically, 5 people were drowned or died as a result of the floods. This could have been far worse, but for the excellent response of the emergency services.

Source: Bye and Horner, 1998, p.16

This is a technical document, but it is also full of issues that are of interest to social scientists. Indeed, the writers of this report are doing a form of social science. It is perhaps important to note that people who call themselves social scientists aren't the only ones doing social science. This is especially the case if you think of social science as a form of investigation, and the social scientist as somebody who resembles a detective or criminal lawyer. Of course, this is not the only or even the best way of describing social science practice, and I don't want to suggest that we all need to imagine ourselves as TV-style detectives. Nevertheless, social science work often involves sorting through a mass of evidence – numerical data, conversations, gestures, written texts, pictures and so on – with the aim of interpreting these materials in order to arrive at an account which offers some form of explanation for the events or phenomena that interest or concern us. The account will normally be accountable to the evidence that we use to construct it (in this way, social scientists often think of themselves as different from writers of fiction, although they can use similar literary devices to very good effect in constructing their accounts, making arguments and so on).

Now, the Environment Agency's preliminary report on the floods in 1998 is a particular kind of account. Its aim is to find a cause or set of causes for the event under investigation. And it is doing a specific kind of job. It is trying to sort through the evidence in order to assign responsibility to various actors in the flood protection system. And it is doing this by *making a fairly clear distinction between social agents on the one hand, and natural agents on the other.*

The most obvious culprit, as far as the Agency is concerned, is the weather. The report argues that a set of unusual atmospheric conditions produced a period and intensity of rainfall for which no-one could have realistically been prepared. Indeed, it suggests that flood defences (for which, remember, the Agency is responsible) are designed to cope with a certain level of river discharge. There is a practical limit to flood protection schemes – any higher and they would be far too expensive and would interfere too much in the normal hydrology of the system. Meanwhile, apart from blaming the freak weather conditions, there is a suggestion that the meteorologists underestimated the rainfall in their forecast. They failed to understand the weather in sufficient detail. This meant that the flood defences and emergency procedures were not as well primed and prepared as they might have been. Of course, the meteorologist would soon defend herself by arguing that there are limits to which a complex, chaotic weather system can be truly known. Again, blame would be shifted on to the weather itself (or perhaps on to El Niño).

Why do you think 'nature' is often blamed for hazards of this kind? Might it be a way of shifting responsibility on to something that can't answer back? Is it a means of hiding human complicity in the production of a disaster? (You may want to return to Box 4.1 to consolidate your views on these questions.)

It is now worth focusing in more detail on the kind of explanation that is being offered. As we have seen, when things go wrong, the search is on for someone or something to blame. In the language that has come to characterize social science, we look for an agent, normally a person or an organization, sometimes a non-human. The agent is someone who or something that we believe has shaped the events that we want to explain. They are, in this version of social science explanation, the prime cause (or prime suspect).

As far as the Environment Agency were concerned, the 1998 floods in England and Wales were to be explained through a 'natural' cause (the weather). This form of explanation is represented in Figure 4.2. Notice how, in this version of events, nature is seen as the cause of society moving from an ordered state to a disordered state.

Notice also that in this form of explanation, nature and society are seen as largely separate categories. Nature visits disorder upon society. This account of the flood presupposes a *purified* view of nature and society (see Figure 1 in the book Introduction). Meanwhile, the form of explanation assumes that there is a clean break between a condition of social order (before the flood)

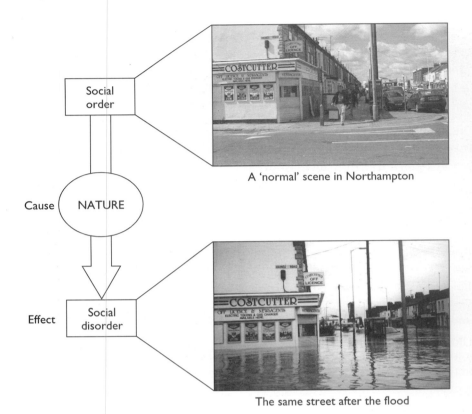

A 'normal' scene in Northampton

The same street after the flood

FIGURE 4.2   The form of explanation used to account for natural disasters

and social disorder (after the flood). Now, in one sense this is self-evident –
and if your home or street were flooded you would agree whole-heartedly
as you set about cleaning up, or restoring order. But, it takes more than
heavy rainfall to produce a flood. The water is not the only guilty party. For
one thing, there needs to be something there to flood. Perhaps planning
regulations were too lax or were ignored so that building could take place
in areas that were liable to flood. Or we could say that the system of land
use was part of the cause of the flood. Too many trees have been removed,
too many smooth surfaces have accompanied urbanization, too many
farmers have ploughed up hedgerows, too many rivers have been
straightened, too many roads, drains and sewers have been built. All of
these activities can speed up the movement of water into the rivers and so
can lead to a rapid and intense build-up of river discharge. If this happens,
the river is unlikely to be able to cope and so bursts its banks. In this case,
the flood is not the fault of nature (or even the weather), it is the specific
mix of the natural and the social that is under suspicion. The hazard has
emerged from the 'interactions between people and environments' (Mitchell
et al., 1989, p.405). It is not simply an external event visited upon a
blameless social order.

FIGURE 4.3 Some land-use changes have tended to increase the rate at which rainwater reaches a river, so increasing the likelihood of flooding

So, rather than seeing disorder being imposed on society, we could argue that the disorder is already there, lurking in the social and natural landscape, well before the actual 'event' or 'disaster'. It is contained within the daily lives of people. The flood could be viewed as an accident waiting to happen, in which case blame has to be distributed more widely. Blame can't rest on the event itself. Causes (like the agricultural system, or, ironically, the over-abstraction of water from rivers and groundwater) will be found before as well as during the flood.

So who or what was to blame? As social scientists we should be suspicious of any attempt to pinpoint any one particular cause, or attribute this to any one particular person or other entity. We are not setting out to find a scapegoat to replace the supernatural (or for that matter the natural). We are not looking for another creature that we can pin the blame upon and hope, rather like the animals that were accused of all manner of crimes in medieval trials, that no-one will care enough about the suspect to question our own motives for assigning responsibility in this way. Instead, it is possible for social scientists to think in more complex ways. We can, as has been suggested throughout this book, begin *to understand the social and the natural as complex, interactive and interrelated matters.*

So where does this leave us? It suggests that we are not looking for absolute causes in social science. Rather, we are interested in a broader understanding of affairs. But this can sound as if social science has no ethics, as if it is missing the tools for deciding that something is right or something is wrong. We can't identify guilty parties from the flow of social and natural activity. Just as we can't blame the weather for floods, likewise we can't blame the regulatory agency (in this case the Environment Agency) because both are operating within a complex world, within which they are partly structured by events beyond their own control. For example, the weather is often not held to be responsible for itself (it is caught up in social activity, as reports of an enhanced greenhouse effect have made clear). Meanwhile, the Environment Agency is caught up in other social worlds (the regulatory system's relationship to the private sector, the willingness or otherwise of people to trust experts and so on) and so-called natural worlds (there *was* a high level of rainfall). Farmers who strip out woodland and hedgerows may be acting in ways that are more or less dictated by the market arrangements that they find themselves in. Indeed, it could seem as though every potentially responsible agent that we identify, upon further analysis, slips from our grasp. They can all claim to be partially determined by the structures within which they are operating. Even El Niño cannot so easily be held to be the prime cause of the floods (see Box 4.1).

This problem can make social scientists very unpopular when they are asked to comment upon a particular problem. It can all too easily sound as though they irresponsibly refuse to find a single cause for something, and thereby end up blaming everything, and ultimately nothing. But before despairing we can try another approach. While realizing that social science is (necessarily) weak at identifying simple causes, it is nevertheless a powerful approach to providing critical interventions that can quickly identify and nullify forms of explanation that are overly simplistic. In this sense, we can be critical, especially when we can spot the 'escape attempts' of those people who may well be at least partially implicated in a matter. In other words, we can use a social science sensitivity to spot inappropriate explanations and suggest that there are social commitments to the accounts that are being offered. So when the buck is being passed, we can be vigilant. In Section 2.2, we shall see how such vigilance can yield a number of insights into the ways in which people and organizations explain and deal with risks and hazards.

FIGURE 4.4   Passing the buck – social scientists can be more vigilant than Steve Bell's policeman

SUMMARY

- In answer to question 1 in the Introduction to this chapter, nature and society are treated as separate in part because there is a tendency to look for simple causes to explain events like hazards. Nature is a favourite scapegoat. It has become the modern equivalent of the 'act of God' explanation for a disaster.

- Natural hazards have social as well as natural causes. They are not external events visited upon people by nature; they emerge from natural and social interactions.

- Social scientists do not always need to look for simple causes. Evidence often points to a more complex picture. Causes are often manifold rather than singular. Social scientists can work with, rather than ignore, such complexity.

2.2 Who benefits from conventional explanations of natural hazards?

The previous subsection established that natural hazards were not simply natural. This statement is underlined as soon as we look to see who and what tend to suffer most after so-called natural disasters. By far the greatest number of deaths associated with natural disasters occurs in those parts of the world where there are profound levels of poverty. This may come as no surprise. Disasters have uneven impacts partly because some locations are more vulnerable than others. Even in the same region, town or village, there are differences in terms of **vulnerability** and impacts.

The poorest, oldest and youngest are often the most vulnerable. In The United States, for example, there is growing evidence that hazard vulnerability divides along lines of race as well as class. Meanwhile there is evidence that it is women and children who bear the greatest burden of environmental threats in many countries (see **Woodward, 2000** for an exposition of these social categories). This is not to suggest that, in talking of vulnerability, we need to assume that certain groups of people, or other living beings, are somehow helpless victims. These patterns of vulnerability are broad, and there are always exceptions where people, plants and animals cope and even flourish despite the odds. Similarly, there is suffering in places where we would not expect vulnerability.

The point that natural hazards affect those who are most vulnerable is central to the case that hazards are socially as well as naturally produced. In this section, we will be exploring why it is that explanations of events that rely solely upon nature as the cause can benefit some groups, and can work to the disadvantage of others. In addition, I will argue that in order to provide alternative explanations of natural hazards we need to look beyond the event itself. We can think about looking beyond a specific event in two, related ways:

1 **Events have histories**. We can look back in time and ask how is it that the people, the land and the environment become so vulnerable? Has there

Vulnerability
Attributes of persons, communities and environments that can increase the potential for suffering from a particular danger or hazardous event.

been mismanagement of resources? Have planning regulations been ignored? Are gender inequalities producing vulnerabilities?

2   **Events have geographies**. We can look at the interactions that are particular to the place where the disaster occurs, and at the interactions that link one place to other places. Is the economic vulnerability of an area produced in part as a result of unfair trade conditions? Has the area been poorly treated by national and international government? Are there firms operating in the area that are neglecting to invest in the essential services that would reduce vulnerability? Are powerful actors actively containing economic and social risks in a specific place?

We can now explore how it is that natural explanations of natural hazards are beneficial to some people and organizations and detrimental to others. Doing so will highlight the uneven distribution of risks and how it is that vulnerability is produced historically and geographically. We shall compare two risk events that occurred within a month of one another.

2.3 Let them eat bananas – the uneven geographies of risk

A tale of two catastrophes

CRISIS IN WALL STREET:
A hedge fund totters and
the West organises
a $3.5bn rescue package

CRISIS IN CENTRAL AMERICA:
At least 11,000 dead, millions
are homeless and the West
organises a $100m rescue package

Traders on Wall Street buying and selling shares in September (left) while two-year old Felix Silva cries at a shelter for evacuees in Nicaragua this week after the disastrous mudslide

FIGURE 4.5   Front-page headline from *The Guardian*, 7 November 1998

The headline in Figure 4.5 reports on two events that occurred in the latter half of 1998. Both can be described as risk events. The response of Western governments was markedly different for the two cases. As the headline indicates, the first situation led to a massive injection of money from wealthy Western banks and government reserves. The second produced a much more modest, some would say derisory, response from the world's wealthier nations.

Here are two ways of accounting for both of these risk events.

2.3.1 Markets and vulnerability

In the previous chapter, you will have appreciated how markets work through the price mechanism. The market model demonstrated that as markets develop there tend to be winners and losers. There is a period of obvious instability as producers go out of business and consumers look for alternatives. Even when markets are well developed, the price mechanism is such that many of the producers and consumers will be operating perilously close to their break-even point. So markets are means of organizing production and consumption in ways that leave economic agents with little room for error. Markets may look to be stable and in equilibrium, but it doesn't take much to throw the whole game into potential chaos.

Given this understanding of markets, we could argue that both of the risk events in Figure 4.5 were generated through market-produced vulnerabilities. The Wall Street crisis was the result of the instability of emerging financial markets in the previously state-planned economies of Eastern Europe and the former Soviet Union. In the run-up to this crisis, financial speculators in New York, London, Tokyo and elsewhere had invested large sums of money into developing markets in these and other so-called emerging economies. The money came from trusts, endowments, shares and pension funds raised in economically wealthy countries (from private pensions, mortgage endowments, individual savings accounts, unit trusts and so on). The assumption was that such funds would produce sizeable profits that could be returned to the companies, share and pension holders in the future. However, market instability made these funds severely vulnerable.

Following the same logic, we could also argue that the Central American crisis was the outcome of the long-term action of worldwide markets for food products like bananas and coffee. Again, it was companies from the world's more powerful economies (especially from the United States) that had large investments in plantations. Following the market model discussed in Chapter 3, we could argue that the markets had produced a particularly vulnerable configuration of nature and society – so much so that the countries of Central America were unprepared for Hurricane Mitch.

Core and periphery
A model used to express the ways in which economic and other forms of power tend to become concentrated in certain places (the core) at the expense of other places (the periphery).

Both events were in part a result of the worldwide financial system. In this respect they had similar histories and geographies. They both involved movements of money between the financial **core** and the financial **periphery** of the world's markets. So why did the two events produce very different reactions from the financial centres in New York? If they were both the result of market failures, why did only one of the events generate a significant rescue package? To understand this we need to mention some of the institutions that surround markets. This brings us to our second take on these risk events.

2.3.2 Uneven vulnerability through risk management

If the production of vulnerability was driven by similar market arrangements that shared similar geographies linking the core and the periphery of the financial system, then the outcomes of those vulnerabilities were very different in terms of their geography. In short, the banking crisis was in danger of spreading like wildfire down the intricate economic networks that link the money in your pocket to stock transactions many thousands of miles away. The Central American crisis was more contained. It looked as though it would have little or no economic effect on most other parts of the world. To understand the wildly divergent responses to these crises, it is useful to consider in some more detail how these two risk events had very different geographies.

The risk returns – dousing down the fire

As the scale of the banking crisis became apparent, a sizeable tranche of Western government money was mobilized in order to bring about some stability and save the financial system. The reasons for such drastic action are worthy of consideration. In one sense the action was taken because the risks had returned to the 'core' of the financial system. And this would have far-reaching repercussions. Not only were the big banks and moneylenders worried, various people in Belfast, Burnley, Elgin, and Aberystwyth may well also have been concerned. In particular, those people who had invested in pensions or other funds, and were soon going to cash those in, were concerned that their financial arrangements might no longer turn out to be what they may have hoped. So the risks had spread out from unstable markets in Russia and elsewhere. They had not been contained. There was a 'boomerang effect'. The fund managers had become caught up and caught out in their own risk-taking venture. Without the kind of action that was taken by the banks and governments, financial insecurity and heightened risk were about to spread like wildfire. Instability would have hit an astonishing number of governments, companies and households. Bear this wildfire geography of risk in mind as we look at the second disaster.

The risk is contained — let the fire burn itself out

In the aftermath of Hurricane Mitch, the devastation in parts of Central America was almost unimaginable. In Honduras alone, upwards of 7,000 people lost their lives. The estimated cost of repairing the damage ran to several billions of dollars. The affected countries of Central America needed to mobilize large amounts of money in order to avert further disasters including disease and total economic collapse.

Now, following the argument that disasters have histories and geographies, we might expect that those partly responsible for the production of vulnerability would be implicated. In the financial crisis discussed above, the venture capitalists were forced to recognize some of their culpability in the production of financial insecurity. They were part of the process that had produced vulnerability and so their own fortunes were locked into the fate of their ventures. However, in the aftermath of Hurricane Mitch, some of the potentially responsible parties squeezed their way out of the situation, seemingly unscathed by the whole affair. This left others to carry the can.

The risk did not spread out in anything like the fashion it had done for the financial crisis. People in Elgin could still buy reasonably priced bananas. Part of the reason for this was that Western interests, in the form of companies operating in the affected states, were rather well protected. And these companies could divert their operations elsewhere with relative ease In doing so, they managed their risk effectively by spreading their production across a number of countries and by making sure that they were adequately insured. Of course, this ability to cope with risk was not shared by all parties concerned. For example, in La Lima, a small northern town of Honduras, the banana plantations that provided a considerable portion of the region's income were buried in mudslides or had been irreparably damaged by floodwater. The crop was destroyed. The plantations would take at least three years to recover. One might think that the large US-owned corporations who control much of the banana trade in this part of Central America would be similarly devastated by the disaster. But, as we have seen, vulnerability to disaster is an uneven matter. In fact, the corporations were insured under an 'act of God' clause. As long as the cause of the disaster was seen as supernatural or natural (or any non-caused cause), their losses would be recovered. The plantation workers were not insured. Furthermore, there is evidence that some of them were soon suspended or laid off by the corporations, who were trying to reduce their costs even further (Davison, 1998). In other words, a different geography of risk from the one that affected the financial institutions was taking shape in the aftermath of Hurricane Mitch. The risk could be contained in Central America. Corporations were powerful enough to shift their investments and responsibilities. They could effectively minimize their risk. This containment and the resulting lack of drastic remedial action served to intensify the danger and vulnerability within Central America.

Partly as a result of this successful risk management and partly as a result of the denial of liabilities that became possible when events were described as natural, the response to the crisis in terms of immediate financial aid was paltry. This was especially the case when compared with the response to the September banking crisis. Even worse, no provision was made to reduce or suspend the debt repayments that the countries of Central America were liable to pay to Western banks. The estimated cost of repayments for Nicaragua and Honduras was £1 million per day. Several development and aid agencies made the metaphorical link between the deaths caused by drowning in the floods and mudslides, and the deaths that were caused by the drowning of the economies of these countries in debt repayments.

ACTIVITY 4.2

Now answer the following questions. You may find it useful to refer back to Sections 2.2 and 2.3 in order to develop your answers:

1 In the aftermath of Hurricane Mitch, who benefited from conventional explanations of natural disasters?

2 How do companies and others manage to avoid risk?

3 Make a list of who or what contributed to the Hurricane Mitch disaster and a separate list of who or what suffered the worst effects. What do these lists tell us about the geographies of vulnerability?

C O M M E N T

1 In the Hurricane Mitch example, the beneficiaries are fairly clear. The large, multinational companies and the debt financiers can both absolve themselves from responsibility for the production of vulnerability. Companies may even turn the disaster to their advantage as they can use it as an excuse to trim their workforce. The attribution of the disaster to natural forces is clearly a way that can be used to obscure the geography and history of vulnerability production. It is a way of de-socializing and therefore depoliticizing the event.

2 The economic risks taken by the corporations in Central America were relatively well controlled. They managed to shift their production interests to other regions, were insured and were able to terminate labour contracts with relative ease. In short, they had made sure that nothing would bind them to the region if things became too unstable. All this careful risk management served to intensify the risks faced by plantation workers.

3 The geography of vulnerability production and the geography of vulnerability are very different. If the crisis in Central America was

produced by many people and organizations over a long period of time and across many countries, then the effects of the crisis were felt by a concentrated group of people in a handful of countries. Figures 4.6(a) and 4.6(b) on pages 134 and 135 are a schematic mapping of the contributions and suffering that can be associated with the disaster.

We have reached the half-way stage in this chapter. Our task so far has been to look at the ways in which natural hazards are explained, and this has suggested some of the ways in which our explanations can contribute to the uneven characteristics of risk. Arguments have also been made about the ways in which social science works. By refusing to accept simple explanations, especially those that load causal responsibility on to 'nature', we have started to produce different takes on the world. As you read the following summary points, you might like to refer back to the first two of the three questions that were posed in the introduction to this chapter.

SUMMARY

- Explanations of natural hazards tend to play down human complicity in an event.

- Calling something natural implies that it is non-social and therefore inevitable, unchangeable and non-political.

- Not only is nature a scapegoat that allows people to cope with the uncertainties of everyday life, but potentially culpable agents benefit from having matters described as natural. It can be a means to shift responsibility away from themselves.

- A social science alternative is to look for the geographies and histories of events, highlighting the interrelations of nature and society – in that way we can start to argue that things are not always inevitable. They might have been, or can be, otherwise.

Our task is now to look at risks and risk taking in some more detail.

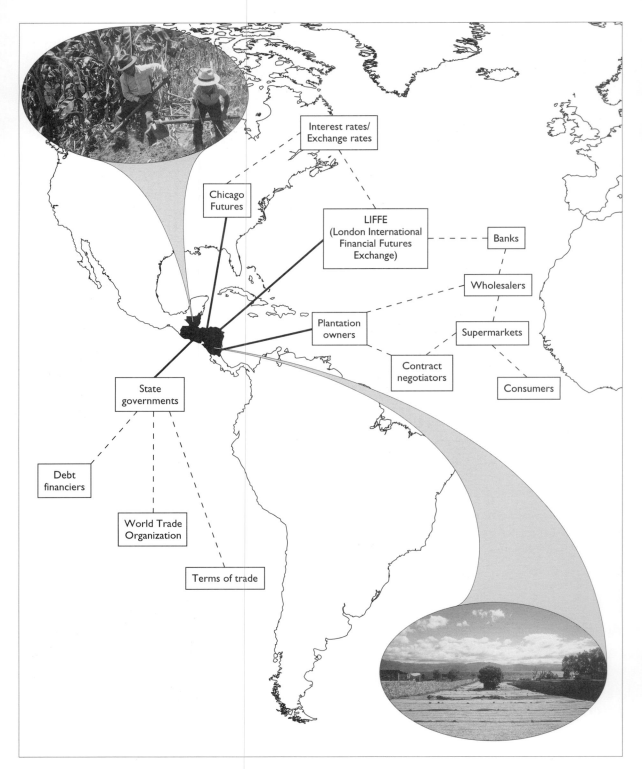

FIGURE 4.6(a)   The production of vulnerability. The diagram represents schematically some of the financial and commodity linkages and connections between the region of Central America and other parts of the world. If the region becomes vulnerable, then these links, along which money and goods will flow, are part of the explanation for the risks

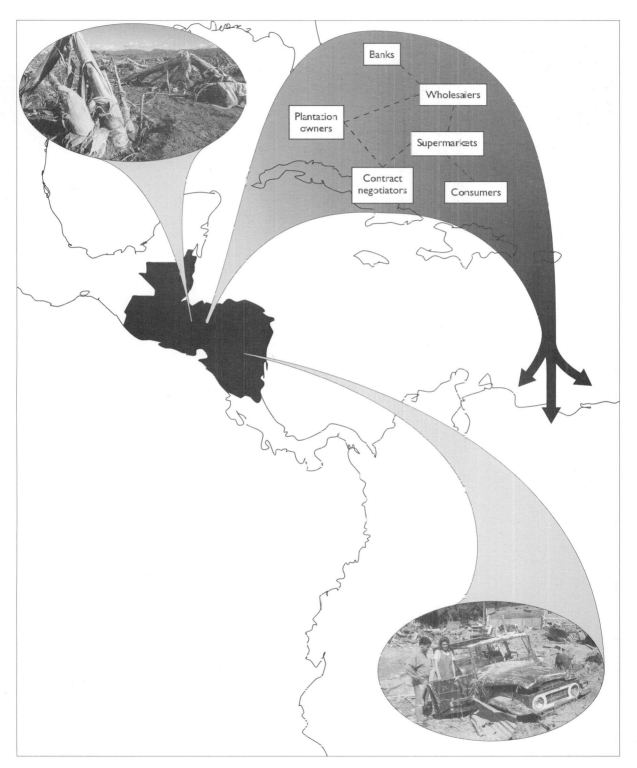

FIGURE 4.6(b) The containment of risk. After the hurricane strikes, some of the contributors to the risk situation are able to extract themselves from the scene. The actions of the plantation owners, other large corporations, supermarkets and so on may mean that consumers in places like Britain need never know that there has been a disaster. The effect in Central America is to increase vulnerability

3   LIVING RISKY LIVES – EATING OUTER NATURE

The workers in Honduras, the plantation owners, the large produce corporations, the fund managers, the banks, governments, mortgage holders and pension contributors, despite all their differences, shared a common characteristic. They all lived with risk. For some social scientists, living with risk has become one of the defining characteristics of our modern, or what some call late modern, times. That is not to say that social scientists would argue that people live riskier lives today than they did in the past. Such an argument would be too general and would not reflect the diversity of risk experiences that we saw in Section 2 of this chapter. So when the German sociologist Ulrich Beck argued, in the late 1980s, that we now live in a **risk society**, he was not making a general case that life was somehow more dangerous today than it was in the past (his argument was published in English in 1992). Rather, the claim was that there had been a qualitative shift in the ways in which people live with risk, and that this shift had occurred, in the main, in the latter half of the twentieth century.

Risk society
An account of modern society emphasizing shifts in the ways in which risk awareness, uncertainty, dependency and trust developed in the twentieth century.

We can summarize these shifts as follows (adapted from Macnaghten and Urry, 1997, p.254):

1   Public awareness of the riskiness of hitherto mundane aspects of daily life has intensified.

2   There has been a growth in the degree of uncertainty that surrounds those risks.

3   People's sense of dependency upon the institutions and expertise responsible for managing and controlling risks has grown.

4   At the same time, the degree of public trust in those institutions and in expertise to manage risks effectively has diminished.

Putting these points together, we can say that in a risk society there is a tendency for debate and contestation over matters that were previously taken for granted or were formerly matters of general agreement. (Think of the various, co-existing conceptions of health that you were introduced to in Chapter 2 as a manifestation of this proliferation of information and argument.) In order to have those debates and to make decisions that were hitherto less likely to be faced as choices, we need more and more information and knowledge. The irony, if it can be called that, is that we need all this knowledge just at a time when many people have started to lose their beliefs and trust. Institutions like organized religion, the family, science, business and government are arguably no longer held in the esteem that they may have once enjoyed. In a risk society, none of these institutions is assumed to have a monopoly on the truth.

Our concern in this section is to understand the relevance of nature–society relations to this risk thesis. Our aim, in particular, is to address the third question that was raised in the introduction to this chapter. As a start, it is worth remembering that in the Central American case risk was intensified in the daily lives of many people. And this intensification was produced when large corporations, debt financiers and others sought to deny their role in producing vulnerability and so deny their responsibility to the affected areas. It was suggested that these denials of responsibility were in part made possible by the ability to separate nature from society in the explanations of disaster and hazard. Furthermore, by ignoring the *social-and-natural* causes of the disaster there was a failure to come to grips with the production of vulnerability. And this might have knock-on effects in the future. Lessons will not have been learned, new appropriate structures will not have been put in place. This and other accidents will continue to wait to happen. It might not be long before even the sophisticated risk management of the international corporations and the insurance industry starts to feel the strain.

Perhaps, therefore, one major cost of trying to hold nature and society apart in our thinking and explaining is the production of more rather than less risk? If this is the case, the suggestion is that it is no longer feasible to treat nature and society as anything other than two sides of the same coin.

We shall now explore the risk society and its relation to questions of nature–society interrelations by focusing on the BSE crisis that developed in Britain in the 1980s and 1990s. We start with some background to this crisis.

3.1 Do cows make you mad?

In this book we have tended to make a simple distinction between inner nature (our genes, organs and our bodies) and outer nature (roughly speaking, our environment). There are times when this distinction seems to make sense. Indeed, it may be one of the issues that we take for granted in our daily lives. But there are times when this convenient division is suddenly and spectacularly undermined. At these moments we realize the extent to which our bodies are intricately wrapped up in broader social and natural worlds. One of these moments was the BSE or 'mad cow' crisis.

For some sections of British society, the Sunday joint of beef has been part of a ritual joining together a wholesome self, the nuclear family and the nation (If you are unsure, think of Beefeaters at the Tower of London and the nickname given to the British people by the French – *les rosbifs*.) For growing children and working men (eating meat has often involved a particular performance of gender), eating beef, and incorporating it into the body, was regarded as an essential part of being morally and physically fit for society. The pure slice of meat was a link between the purity and bounty of the land, the family kitchen and the healthy, working body. To be sure, this comfortable world has been punctured a number of times before. Excessive

FIGURE 4.7 A 'traditional' scene: a family sitting down to Sunday roast beef and trimmings

eating of red meat has been linked to dietary disorders and heart disease for many years. Likewise, there have been many campaigns to raise public awareness of intensive farming and animal suffering, particularly with respect to veal production. So concerns were already in place. But the BSE crisis seemed to bring these and other concerns together. As a result, many commentators have argued that the significance of eating beef – and indeed the public view of the food production industry, science and government – changed substantially in the wake of the crisis.

The desperate images of diseased cows, disoriented, frightened and stumbling across farmyards, tapped into a general concern over modern industrial agriculture. Something was very wrong. This was a moment at which people could no longer so easily forget where their food came from. Beef products did not just come from the supermarket, surrounded by advertising images of contented cows re-enacting a scene from *The Sound of Music*. The beef product had a more complex history and geography, including a countryside and an agricultural system which looked increasingly unlike the idyllic rural images that represented Old England. The intensive rearing of cows, the protein-enriched feed containing rendered animal products, the slaughterhouses and rendering plants that processed animal carcasses at astonishing rates, were matters that were all brought to the public's attention. And they were all matters that many meat-eaters would have preferred not to think about. Indeed, the entire food production system shifted from being taken for granted (and possibly being viewed somewhat romantically) to being a cause for general concern. As it did so, the relationship between inner and outer nature was thrown into relief. At the same time, both of these 'natures' were shown to be unavoidably linked to a huge and profitable industry, replete with competing interests. Beef products had connected nature and society for a long time. After BSE, any public fears regarding these connections were intensified.

FIGURE 4.8   Images of the food industry changed during the BSE crisis – an abattoir worker 'processing' a carcass

At one level there was a simple though crucial question that the government and the public were asking in the late 1980s and 1990s 'Is beef safe to eat?' The question referred to the possibility that the eating of BSE-infected beef products might induce a variant of Creutzfeldt-Jakob Disease (CJD – the human equivalent of BSE) in human beings. It also referred to the efforts being made to exclude infected products from the food chain. This matter was by no means straightforward in an industry that was technologically set up to process dead animals at high speed and to use virtually every 'component' of the carcass. BSE was also likely to be carried by animals not showing clinical symptoms. There was no known test that would identify carriers of the disease. Even the initial cause and the identity of the disease carrier or agent were the subject of disagreements. So sorting out infected stock from 'clean' stock, and good meat from bad meat, became huge logistical and practical problems for the industry.

ACTIVITY 4.3

Look back to the four characteristics of a risk society that were set out at the start of Section 3. Concentrating for the moment on the first three points, to what extent do you think the BSE crisis is representative of a risk society issue?

COMMENT

In many ways the BSE crisis seems to provide plenty of evidence for the risk society. We can take each point in turn.

1   Eating beef was once an activity that was largely taken for granted. It was part of a routine, wrapped up in ideas about nationhood, religion and identity. The BSE crisis threatened this comfortable existence. Traditions as well as health now seemed to be at risk. These concerns were not necessarily new. They were, however, undoubtedly intensified during the crisis.

2   The risks associated with eating beef were difficult to judge; no-one knew what was causing the disease. Other uncertainties included: whether or not the disease could jump species and infect human beings; whether or not cows could be diagnosed in time to remove them from the food system; whether the meat industry could adjust its methods to minimize the risk to humans.

3   Dependency upon scientific expertise and upon governmental institutions was pronounced. BSE-infected meat was not something that anyone could detect. It did not smell or look any different from safe beef. Many cows may well have carried the disease without showing symptoms. Scientific expertise was therefore necessary to provide diagnoses and develop knowledge on the causes and effects of the disease. Government was relied upon to provide the right kind of restrictions and policies to manage the crisis. The agricultural system and the food industry were relied upon to implement policies effectively.

We can now look more closely at the fourth characteristic of a risk society, that of declining trust. I will do this by focusing upon how certain prominent experts dealt with the crisis, followed by an assessment of how their pronouncements on the risks of eating beef were treated by the public.

SUMMARY

- A number of sociologists have argued that broad cultural changes have produced a society where risk has become a more prominent issue in people's lives.

- A risk society is characterized by a change in public awareness, a growth in uncertainty, a growth in dependency on experts and a reduction in the level of trust in expertise.

- The BSE crisis involved a qualitative change in people's attitude to food, a high level of uncertainty and an increased sense of dependency upon expert systems and institutions.

3.2 What the experts said

In a risk society it is assumed that people will, initially at least, turn to expert institutions in order to receive assurances or otherwise on a threat or hazard. In this section we look at three 'expert statements'. The aim is to pick out some of the characteristics of expert statements in order that we may understand how they were received (or why some of them were ignored) by the public.

ACTIVITY 4.4

Read the extracts in Reading 4.2. As you read each extract, try to summarize the position that was being taken on the risk of BSE being transmitted to humans. In particular, you should note down:

1   What level of risk was assumed by each of the writers – how safe did they think it was for people to eat beef?

2   How certain were the writers of their risk calculations?

3   Why do you think there are differences between the three statements? Are there any similarities?

The government scientist

Mr Keith Meldrum, Head of the Ministry of Agriculture Veterinary Service, said the risk of the disease being transmitted from cattle to humans could not be completely discounted, but emphasized that it was only a remote possibility. [...] The Government's measures were more than adequate to remove what was 'probably a zero risk' to consumers:

> I am totally content that what we are doing now is totally sound and is all that we need to do in order to remove any possibility of BSE exposure to man [sic] from cattle. However, I cannot say there is no risk to man from BSE. It is too early. We have only had this disease in this country for three years and the incubation period in man in cases of encephalopathies is very long indeed.

Source: Keith Meldrum, Chief Veterinary Officer, Ministry of Agriculture, Fisheries and Food, quoted in *The Times*, 22 January 1990 (also cited at the BSE Inquiry, 19 October 1998)

The government minister

As the chief medical officer has confirmed, British beef can continue to be eaten safely by everyone, adults and children.

We have taken action to deal with the public health concerns and the animal health aspect of BSE on the basis of the best independent scientific advice.

Source: John Gummer, Minister of Agriculture, Fisheries and Food, 18 May 1990, quoted in *The Times* (also cited in Irwin, 1995, pp.21 and 23)

The dissenting scientists

Man [sic] may not be vulnerable. There is no data on which to make a prediction. The best result would be no effect at all; the worst could be the development of Creutzfeldt-Jakob Disease on a massive scale 20–30 years hence. This could be followed by vertical transmission in man. [...] There seems little prospect of these uncertainties being clarified by research over the next few years.

Source: Professor Richard Lacey and Dr Stephen Dealler, June 1990, Report to the UK Parliamentary Agriculture Committee (cited in Lacey, 1994, p.106)

C O M M E N T

First of all, I will deal with the differences amongst the three statements (including my thoughts on questions 1 and 2) and then follow this by looking at the similarities.

Expert differences

When I looked at the three accounts I was struck that they were all ostensibly talking about the same thing, and yet there were some glaring differences in the ways in which they understood the risks. The government scientist suggested that the risk was so small as not to be worth considering, although there was an admission that he might be wrong. The minister suggested that there was no risk whatsoever, everything was under control. There was no expression of doubt. Finally, the dissenting scientists suggested that the risks were at that time unknowable. There was therefore a chance that the risks were very high. The only thing that they were certain of was that there was currently uncertainty in any future prediction.

The reasons for the differences in the accounts of risk provided by these people can partly be linked to their different social positions. The government minister was concerned that any message expressing doubt or uncertainty, even if it was only a hint that there might be a minute risk, would be seized upon by the press, by consumers and by foreign competitors. He was critical of Keith Meldrum for even mentioning the possibility of risk in press interviews. Both men were under intense pressure from the agricultural lobby and from the Department of Trade and Industry to say the right things in public. British exports were at stake. There was a good deal of money on the line (the export trade in beef was worth roughly £500 million), not to mention Britain's international reputation. So, in this sense, Meldrum and Gummer's statements were fairly similar. They were both of a mind to believe the risk assessments and interpret any residual uncertainties as irrelevant. The difference was that Meldrum felt bound to express a small, residual doubt. He was not only committed to the farming industry, having to represent their interests in his press statements, but he was also bound to the conventions of science. His argument therefore included the cautionary note that all the evidence was not yet available. There were more questions to ask, and more answers to find. Gummer was less impressed by this argument. He was more interested in answers than questions. He had to make decisions on the basis of the 'best independent scientific advice' (he could have added 'currently available', but did not do so – such an admission would have undermined his case). This was his reasoning: there was no scientific evidence that BSE in cattle was reaching human beings through oral consumption; therefore there was no risk.

Lacey and Dealler's reasoning was more akin to Meldrum's than it was to Gummer's. To paraphrase their position: while it was granted that there was no evidence that BSE was reaching human beings through oral consumption or that resulting infection could lead to development of CJD, that was not to say that evidence would not be found in the future. Lacey and Dealler suggested that 'no data' was indicative of the lack of good research in this area and not an excuse for limited action. Whilst they were not aware of any evidence that proved that humans were at risk, they argued that there was also no evidence that humans were *not* at risk. More time and resources were needed to carry out research into this matter. Until then, we should act as if there was a high risk. We needed to act with *precaution*. A **precautionary approach to risk** was justified, they were arguing, because even a small chance of being wrong was still a chance that could lead to a catastrophe. It wasn't right to ignore the chance given these potentially catastrophic circumstances.

Expert similarities

The first similarity that I spotted in the three accounts was that they all referred to science. This is perhaps not surprising. Scientific approaches to risk assessment have traditionally been the preferred policy tool of British government in food and other kinds of risk events. Indeed, when the UK government sought advice on the BSE crisis it relied solely upon scientific opinion and committees made up of medical, veterinary and zoological specialists.

The second similarity is harder to spot. It relates to the understanding of uncertainty. The statements all give the impression that with more science and technology we would progressively remove the uncertainties. That is, *uncertainty and risk were thought of as temporary matters*: with more research any residual doubt would be progressively eliminated. The assumption of all the writers was that scientific evidence would be built up by conducting experiments on laboratory animals in order to understand more about the infectious properties of the disease agent and about the development of the disease in mammals. The risks would not only become known (through ever more sophisticated experiments), they would also become *predictable*. They could then be minimized by applying more technical expertise to the problem. The latter would involve placing new restrictions on farming and food-processing activities. In the BSE case, this

Precautionary approach to risks
Acting with care, especially when there is a lack of agreement on the outcomes of an action. This may involve taking a more expensive action in the short term to reduce the risk of paying a high amount later.

procedure involved experimental feeding trials to determine the infectivity of various parts of a diseased cow. The results of the trials suggested that certain parts of infected cows were more infectious than others. A policy was then formulated which stipulated that various cuts of beef be removed from the food system (so-called 'specified bovine offal', initially including the spine and head of the cow).

In sum, scientific research, combined with better technical management of the food system, allowed successive agriculture ministers and ministry scientists to argue that 'progress' was being made. The main disagreement in terms of the three statements that we have looked at here was about the rate of that progress.

Contrary to the second characteristic of the risk society described at the start of Section 3, we could say that the experts largely thought that any growth in uncertainty around the matter of eating beef was a temporary matter. For these people, modern science and technology could still be relied upon to produce a more certain world. In Section 3.3 we shall see that all parties in the BSE crisis did not necessarily share this faith in science and technology.

SUMMARY

- Experts representing science and government differed in their opinions as to the risk of contracting CJD from British beef.

- The government expressed the risk as zero, partly in an attempt to reduce the public concern and protect the market in beef.

- Scientists continued to express uncertainty, although they disagreed over the relative importance of the uncertainties.

- Despite their differences, government and scientific experts were of the opinion that, in time, the risks could be determined and controlled. Uncertainty was a temporary matter that would be progressively removed with more research and better policies. The government put a good deal of faith in natural science as a means to develop policy.

3.3 Rationalities and cultures of risk

Despite the repeated assurances from government ministers and their scientific advisors that 'in the normal sense of the term' eating beef was 'safe', there remained a high level of discomfort with respect to the risks of eating beef in Britain. Local councils took beef off the menu in schools, and large restaurant and fast food chains made it known that they were sourcing their beef from outside the UK. Many consumers sought out alternatives and beef prices collapsed. The government and its advisors labelled this behaviour as irrational. They accused the public of being misinformed and of not understanding the science (for an account, see Wynne, 1996a). In this section, we shall look more closely at what was labelled as rational and irrational in the crisis. I will argue that the public understanding of the issues was far from being inferior to that of science.

ACTIVITY 4.5

Do you think it is irrational to take some large risks whilst refusing to take what look as though they are much smaller risks? Under what circumstances might you regard this behaviour as entirely reasonable? Compare eating beef with using mobile telephones (with its radiation risk), playing dangerous sports and drinking alcohol.

COMMENT

I will limit my answer to a comparison with mobile telephones. According to the scientific risk assessments, the statistical probability of suffering a radiation-associated illness as a result of using a mobile phone is higher than the risk of developing CJD by eating beef. So why did people buy mobile phones in abundance in the 1990s, while often choosing not to eat beef? One answer is that the benefits of mobile phones may be regarded as far outweighing the potential health risks. People often say that once they have become used to having a mobile phone they feel lost without it. Many people, and many women in particular, feel safer with a mobile phone if they are travelling alone. The more significant risk for them is the physical danger that seems to be partly reduced by being able to stay in touch. So people may *trade off* one risk for another (Wylie, 1998).

In contrast to mobile phone use, people found it fairly straightforward to avoid British beef by choosing alternatives. They could eat chicken, pork, purchase Irish or other beef products, or turn vegetarian. So, even though the risk from eating beef was reportedly very small, it was for many people not worth taking. There is nothing irrational in avoiding minute risk if adjustments to eating habits or behaviour can be made with very little effort or disruption.

How does this sound? Does this reflect your thoughts on Activity 4.5? Is this how you shop? Do you make choices like this, trading risks off, one with another, and considering alternative products? Some people undoubtedly spend a good deal of time deciding how best to spend their money. And there can be little doubt that people do consider health matters seriously. But perhaps we shouldn't be carried away with the idea that a risk society leads to everyone becoming more calculating, making individual, rational choices. Many people feel either that they don't have that much of a choice, or that they buy things and do things without really giving it a second thought. In many ways, the scientific probabilities and risk calculations just don't seem that relevant to people's lives. This brings us to another set of ideas as to why the government's assurances on the safety of beef (and for that matter on genetically-modified foodstuffs or on other issues of the day) were largely ignored. These ideas are less to do with people making individual risk decisions. Instead, they address what might be a called a *cultural shift*.

Earlier I suggested that the crucial question with respect to the BSE crisis was, 'Is beef safe to eat?' The idea that I want to pursue now is that people soon tired of this question – there were too many opinions around to make a useful decision, and people did not have the time to consider all the issues. So the question changed. It became, *'Do we trust these people with the food that we put into our bodies?'*

Structure of feeling
The culture of the period that structures, but is in turn structured by, people's experiences and actions. It is used to take us away from an account of action based on individual agents or on overarching structures.

This question speaks less about individual risk calculations and more about a general **structure of feeling** regarding food, science and government. In particular, the question signals a general discomfort with the risk-assessment culture that informed the way the government handled the risks. This governmental risk culture was based on a rather narrow form of scientific rationality, which saw nature and society as essentially separate matters. The assumption was that scientists could make observations concerning the nature of the disease. These observations could then be turned into knowledge which would be *relevant* to the rest of society. Elsewhere, and outside this governmental risk culture, society and nature were rarely treated as such separable matters. Indeed, many people assessed risk statements (like 'beef is safe to eat') more in terms of who was making the statement than the actual statement itself (for an extended treatment of this argument, see Wynne, 1996b). In other words, people did not make a distinction between a physical risk and the institution that was supposedly in charge of operations. If the latter was found wanting, then people assumed that the risks could get out of hand. In this alternative culture of risk and mistrust, nature and society are regarded as two sides of the same coin. The next subsection focuses on just how the government managed to misjudge this structure of feeling by relying upon a limited sense of (physical or natural) risk.

3.3.1 The reliance on science and the failure to generate trust

Many assessments of risks to human health are based upon animal experiments, 80 per cent of which, in Britain at least, are carried out on mice and rats. There are many ethical considerations connected to animal experiments. These are complex arguments in themselves and cannot be covered in detail in this chapter. However, there are some arguments over the nature of the evidence that such experiments can be expected to produce which can be considered here.

ACTIVITY 4.6

Read the following text which has been used in promotional information produced by the organization Animal Aid. After you have read the text, write a list of reasons why you think that calculations of health risks to humans based on laboratory experiments on animals may result in either incorrect or only approximate human health risk assessments.

> If we relied on laboratory rats, for instance, much medical knowledge would be turned on its head: thalidomide would be considered safe; alcohol would be regarded as no more toxic to the liver than sugar; TB would not be considered a dangerous disease since rats are hardly affected. Smoking would not be held responsible for lung cancer; doctors would reject evidence that oral contraceptives increase the risk of blood clots because in rats they have totally the opposite effect; and we wouldn't consider it necessary to have vitamin C in our diet.
>
> (Summary, from the Animal Aid website (http://www.animalaid.org.uk/), of scientific evidence presented in Sharpe, 1994)

COMMENT _____

When I thought about it, and considered some of the arguments in Chapter 1 of this book on the similarities and differences between and within species, I became increasingly doubtful as to the relevance of the evidence that is produced through animal experimentation. The degree of match between the social and biological lives of small laboratory mammals, kept in cages, usually only for a matter of months, and the lives of over 6 billion human beings seems, at best, approximate. Unlike the laboratory animals, human beings:

- may live long and complex lives;

- will undoubtedly be exposed to all manner of different chemicals, other organisms and physical processes over long periods of time;

- may have particular biological and social characteristics (including allergies, habits like smoking and drinking, experience of pregnancy, and so on).

_____

Your list may contain these and other points. The main issue is that risk assessments based upon laboratory tests are not easily translated to the outside world. Any statement that suggests that the risks that have been determined in a laboratory are equivalent to those that exist elsewhere is itself based on a questionable set of assumptions. At the root of these assumptions is a purified approach to nature and society. The suggestion is that if we can describe the *nature* of a risk then this description will hold whatever the social conditions. Unfortunately, and as has been stressed throughout this book, it is not so straightforward to hold society and nature apart. Any measurement of nature is, in the non-purified world that we have described in this book, a measurement of a particular natural-and-social interrelationship. We can emphasize this point by looking at laboratory science in a little more detail.

Many scientific and technical risk assessments are carried out by simplifying as much as possible of the world in order to concentrate on the processes that cause harm. This is a form of modelling, similar in some senses to the method that you were introduced to in the previous chapter. In order to arrive at a definite answer regarding the hazardous *nature* of a material (like tissue infected with the BSE agent), experimenters try to make sure that no other element of the laboratory environment could cause a reaction or effect. By repeating the experiment with different concentrations of infectious material (or doses), this simplified world also allows the practitioner to identify safe exposure levels. With further analysis, the mechanisms and processes that lead from exposure to illness can be mapped.

Two forms of uncertainty become important when this model of risk is interpreted. *First*, there is always the chance that the knowledge produced in the laboratory may be wrong. Not everything can be controlled and laboratory workers continually have to make difficult interpretations of their results (a slight change in colour, a subtle movement on a screen or a small change in correlation results). Nevertheless, in time, these kinds of uncertainties may well be reduced (but cannot be fully eliminated) as the experiments are repeated. The *second* form of uncertainty arises when this knowledge is used to make predictions about risks in different environments (outside the laboratory). Whilst the risk knowledge in the laboratory may be fairly robust, as soon as we step outside the uncertainties multiply. The experiment is no longer controlled. We are invariably talking about worlds that are infinitely more complex on account of immense natural and social diversity (a point that is emphasized in Activity 4.6).

This radical, or permanent, version of uncertainty does not imply that laboratory or any other form of scientific knowledge is worthless. But it does imply that if knowledge is to be useful, its own limitations must be recognized. Unfortunately, as feminist scholars and sociologists of science have repeatedly pointed out, laboratory science is often confusingly assumed (more often by politicians than scientists) to provide explanations of nature that are applicable everywhere and at all times. Rather than accepting the knowledge produced as a worthwhile explanation of the world under particular (and possibly peculiar) natural and social conditions (those of the laboratory), the knowledge is elevated to being *the* definitive version of affairs. The laboratory model is confused for reality. It is assumed that the model can access a purified version of nature, whereas it more correctly speaks of a simplified set of natural and social interactions.

It is the simplifications that underlie this form of knowledge that become absolutely evident when such knowledge is used to make assurances on risk to the general public. So, when the agriculture minister claimed that he had acted in accordance with the best independent scientific advice, many people were not impressed. Likewise, when these risk assessments of the infectivity of various bovine tissues were used to formulate a strategy of risk management in the food industry, a number of gross assumptions concerning natural and social interrelationships in the food system were made. As Macnaghten and Urry (1997, p.256) describe it, 'Official policy took for granted, *inter alia*, that farmers would comply with official regulations, the abattoir workers would carefully and systematically remove SBO [specified bovine offal] from animal carcasses, and that feed manufacturers would discard mammalian offal in cattle feed.' Given the public understanding of the workings of such a large industry where an international market continually squeezed profit margins, these assumptions seemed at best unlikely and at worst negligent. These kinds of assumptions reinforced a general mistrust of institutions and scientific expertise, especially when the latter were shown to rely upon what people recognized as oversimplifications of social and natural interrelations.

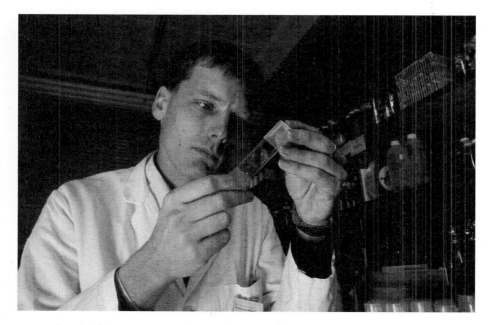

FIGURE 4.9 Science – a practice you can trust?

To be sure, these feelings of mistrust had been around for a long time. Scientists have long been seen, perhaps unfairly, as rather narrow in focus, unable to understand the complexities of social and natural situations (think of the 'bumbling boffin' image that is often portrayed in popular media). Similarly, politicians have long been regarded as capable of being far from independent and getting themselves caught up in various crimes and misdemeanours. But feelings of scepticism were undoubtedly given new impetus during the BSE scare when time and again scientists and government ministers argued that eating beef was safe, only to be faced with growing evidence that their risk calculations and their policies were insufficient. This intensification of mistrust in the general area of food provision continued for some time. So the question shifted from, 'Is beef safe to eat?' to, 'Do we trust government, science and industry with our food?' Furthermore, this was not a question that was asked by every individual as they made decisions on whether or not to eat beef. Rather, the question circulated in the media, in living rooms, in pubs, in schools. It took on a general level of importance. It became part of a structure of feeling. Finally, this structure of feeling would have important effects on the ways in which debates over the acceptability of genetically-modified organisms in food production would be conducted in Britain in the late 1990s and beyond (see **Allen, 2000**).

The BSE example considered in Section 3 is in many ways symptomatic of a risk society. In Section 3.3, I have extended the description of a risk society by highlighting two significant aspects of the BSE crisis:

1   The crisis involved an intensification of mistrust in institutions and expertise.

2   The intensification of mistrust was partly partly a result of the government's reliance upon a form of logic that treated nature and society as separate matters.

The issue was not that a growth in risk and expert disagreements led to the public losing their trust in science and expertise. The risks of eating meat became less relevant as time went on and the trust was not necessarily there in the first place. Rather, it is evident that the government failed to build up trust by relying upon a form of management that, in neglecting to admit uncertainty where necessary, was alien to most people's experiences and lives.

SUMMARY

● The British government's approach to risk has been to shift responsibility for decision-making on to science. In doing so it failed to recognize the limitations of relying upon a small number of specialized fields of knowledge.

● The government and their scientists interpreted the public's mistrust as irrational and ill-informed, when it is likely that people's everyday understanding of risk was just as sophisticated as theirs, if not more so.

● The rational decision making preferred by the government neglected the permanent forms of uncertainty associated with a diverse natural-and-social world. The government confused laboratory knowledge with natural reality.

● I have argued that laboratory knowledge is a description of a particular set of natural–social interrelations. Its applicability is founded on recognizing these simplifications and not on forgetting that they exist (a forgetting that is accomplished when the science is presented as describing nature and nature alone).

- In dealing with risk, people are less likely to make individual calculations, but rather contribute to a more general culture of trust and mistrust. Social scientists therefore need to think in ways that are not always based upon 'individual' agency. Structure of feeling is one way of bringing structure and agency together in a social science analysis.

4 CONCLUSION

I started this chapter by asking three questions. If you now return to those questions you should be able to offer detailed responses. My comments on the three questions are given below.

1 *If society and nature are no more than two sides of the same coin, why do we often talk as if they are separate matters?*

This question can be answered using the work on natural hazards. Disasters and hazards were shown to be the result of natural-and-social interrelationships. Any description that attempts to purify this mixture by labelling it 'nature' is either a poor description or it is one that is attempting to take someone or something out of the frame of responsibility. Attributing an event to nature can therefore be a political move.

The question can also be answered by referring to the BSE case. One example would be that, by treating the disease as a matter for natural science, the government could refrain from saying anything about the wider issues concerning the morality and sustainability of the intensive industrialization of food.

2 *What do we gain and what do we lose by holding nature and society apart like this in our thoughts?*

As we saw in the Central American case, certain people gain and certain people lose when nature and society are treated as poles apart. More generally, we have argued that the insistence on treating nature and society as separate matters can serve to intensify feelings of risk and feelings of mistrust. The BSE crisis illustrates this matter only too well.

3 *Can we carry on for much longer thinking that society and nature are essentially amenable to separation?*

My answer to this question is, 'Probably not.' The separation of nature and society is starting to cause more problems than it is solving. To be sure, this purified version of the world can help governments make simplifications that can facilitate decision making, but the costs of such simplifications can be profound. Likewise, corporations can benefit from separating nature and society, but if the real causes of disasters like Hurricane Mitch and BSE are thereby not confronted then the gains that are made may only be short-lived. It is for reasons like these that social scientists like Beck and others that you read about in this chapter have called for new forms of decision-making and new institutional frameworks. The next book in this series (**Hughes and Fergusson, 2000**) takes on some of these issues.

REFERENCES

Allen, J. (2000) 'Power: its institutional guises (and disguises)' in *Ordering Lives: Family, Work and Welfare*, London, Routledge/The Open University.

Beck, U. (1992) *Risk Society,* London Sage.

Bye, P. and Horner, M. (1998) *Easter Floods 1998: Preliminary Assessment By The Independent Review Team, Report To The Board Of The Environment Agency*, England, Environment Agency.

Davison, P. (1998) 'No bananas, no homes, little hope', *The Independent*, 15 November, p.16.

Hughes, G. and Ferguson, R. (eds) (2000) *Ordering Lives: Family, Work and Welfare*, London, Routledge/The Open University.

Irwin, A. (1995) *Citizen Science: A Study of People, Expertise And Sustainable Development,* London, Routledge.

Lacey, R. (1994) *Mad Cow Disease,* Jersey, Cypsela.

Mitchell, J.K., Devine N. and Jagger K. (1989) 'A contextual model of natural hazard', *Geographical Review,* vol.79, no.4, pp.391–409.

Macnaghten, P. and Urry, J. (1997) *Contested Natures*, London, Routledge.

Sharpe, R. (1994) *Science on Trial,* Sheffield, Awareness Publishing.

Woodward, K. (ed.) (2000) *Questioning Identity: Gender, Class, Nation*, London, Routledge/The Open University.

Wylie, I. (1998) 'Mad cows and Englishmen' in Ratzan, S. (ed.) *The Mad Cow Crisis: Health And The Public Good,* London, UCL Press.

Wynne, B. (1996a) 'Patronizing Joe public', *Times Higher Education Supplement*, 12 April, p.13.

Wynne, B. (1996b) 'May the sheep safely graze' in Lash, S., Szerszynski, B. and Wynne, B. (eds) *Risk, Environment and Modernity: Towards a New Ecology* (Theory, Culture and Society), London, Sage.

FURTHER READING

Hewitt, K. (1997) *Regions Of Risk: A Geographical Introduction To Disasters*, London, Longman. This provides a thorough review of the hazards research literature in geography and other disciplines. The book is also excellent with respect to the differences between technical and more cultural notions of risk and vulnerability.

Irwin, A. (1995) *Citizen Science: A Study Of People, Expertise And Sustainable Development*, London, Routledge. On risk and science, this provides a thoughtful and clear introduction to the complexities of science and society. The book also makes a useful case for institutional change and more publicly informed modes of decision making in the environmental sphere.

Macnaghten, P. and Urry, J. (1997) *Contested Natures*, London, Routledge. Macnaghten and Urry provide a comprehensive and clearly written book on nature and society issues, including an excellent section on risk society issues.

Ratzan, S. (ed.) (1998) *The Mad Cow Crisis: Health And The Public Good*, London, UCL Press. For those who would like to know more about the BSE case, this volume includes a variety of takes on the crisis.

Afterword

Steve Hinchliffe

From our opening examples of cloning and landscapes, to our engagement
with intelligence, health, economies and environmental risks, we have
confronted a social and natural world that looks impure; that is, we have
repeatedly found that those aspects of our lives that look to be purely natural
turn out, upon closer inspection, to have social dimensions. For example, if
we isolated DNA in a test tube, there would be little sign of intelligence. For
the latter to be produced we need a complex set of interactions, which would
include DNA but would not be reducible to chemical formulae. Similarly, we
have met with situations that we have been used to calling entirely social but
which are also dependent upon mixtures of social and natural worlds. The
economy, and in particular markets, are good examples of social institutions
that result in distributions of goods and services which have implications that
are not only social. Markets will tend towards creating a situation where costs
are externalized on to zero-priced nature. However, the idea of using nature
as a dumping ground for our unwanted by-products in order to save on
narrowly defined economic costs has become more and more untenable. The
despoiling of land, water and air is starting to have social effects. So we are
beginning to realize that we cannot alter nature without having effects upon
society. Time and again the modern myth that we can hold society and nature
apart starts to falter.

This cross-cutting of society and nature is very different from the purified
forms that were referred to in the Introduction to this book (see Figure 1 in
the Introduction). Diagrammatically, we have moved from thinking of nature
and society as distinct realms or regions to thinking of them as interlaced or
entangled. One way of redrawing this figure would be to make the circles
overlap. Another, perhaps more graphically interesting, way would be to
draw a tangled web or network. No matter which thread you follow, be it
social or natural, you will always become entangled in other social and
natural networks and threads (see Figure 1).

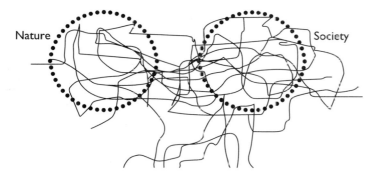

FIGURE 1 Nature and
society entangled
Source: based on Latour,
993, Figure 4.3.4, p.102

The initial aim of this book was to demonstrate that nature and society exist in mixes. A second aim was to establish the importance of re-thinking nature and society at a time of increased uncertainty and risk. Our third aim was to demonstrate the skills and resources available to social scientists when confronting nature and society questions. In order to emphasize some of the progress that has been made in the foregoing chapters it will be useful briefly to consider three social science themes that have informed the writing of the chapters of this book. The themes are, structure and agency, uncertainty and diversity, knowledge and knowing.

Structure and agency

The theme of structure and agency runs throughout the book and helps us to understand human identity and intelligence, health and illness, market behaviour and environmental protection, and people's reaction to risks and hazards.

A common assumption made by many people is that we (and for that matter all species) are in some way structured by our biology (our inner nature). We are born, we live and we die as a result of the genetic inheritance we have received from our parents and, more generally, from millions of years of evolution. Now, in some senses it would be facile to try to deny that each of us is equipped with different sets of possibilities, and we are undoubtedly, from time to time, constrained by our biological inheritance. But, as Steve Hinchliffe and Judith Greene suggested in Chapter 1, it would also be far too simplistic, and at the same time politically questionable, to suggest that we are biological machines living out a preprogrammed life over which we have little or no control. In suggesting this, we would be in danger of underestimating the role that our social and natural environments play in deciding whether or not and how a gene works. Furthermore, we would also neglect to say anything of the ways in which human beings (like all species) play a role in shaping those environments. As the biologist Steven Rose puts it, 'Organisms ... are far from passive – not just we humans, but all other living forms as well – are active players in their own futures' (1997, p.141). This sense of the active also gives us room to explore the *politics* of agency and structure. If structures do not wholly determine what we do and who we are, then we open up the possibility for changing things. This does not mean the human mind can escape its biological, cultural, material and social settings, but it does mean that those settings are not necessarily fixed and there will be possibilities for different forms of action. Bringing the social and natural together, then, helps us to unhinge both realms from the language of fixity whilst recognizing that neither offers us unending sources of possibility.

In the same way that our inner nature both constrains and enables human action (demonstrating that agency and structure are always dependent upon one another), so too do outer nature and society. We saw, for example, in

Chapter 2, how our health was structured in complex ways by our biology interacting with social matters such as race, class, place, income, housing, and general well-being. Such structures are not fixed, so Brenda Smith and David Goldblatt explored some of the ways in which they offered political resources for dealing with health and ill-health. The interrelations between agency and structure were readily apparent in Chapter 3. As economic agents actively respond to price signals, so a market emerges which not only shapes future actions (it acts as a strongly influential structure) but also enables change and innovation (more agency). So the question is posed, can markets allow us to innovate in such a way as to build an environmentally less risky future? For Sue Himmelweit and Roberto Simonetti the jury has to be out, because markets both enable and constrain. Markets offer, through the price mechanism, some of the most promising means for dealing with environmental degradation. Adjusting the money values placed, or not placed, on the environment could help to shift priorities and remove the tendency to treat nature as an external aspect of economic affairs. But, at the same time, markets confine us to what seem to be some politically unassailable positions. The more we place monetary values on nature, the more the world (and more of the world) becomes subject to the dictates of economic rules and distributions. How environments will respond to being structured in this way is a matter for intense political debate. Finally, Chapter 4 warned against treating outer nature as an absolute structure that would allow us to ignore the role of human agency in the production of environmental disasters. If the social and natural are entangled, then human responsibility for vulnerability cannot be so easily ignored.

Uncertainty and diversity

In terms of our individual and species characteristics, of our health and welfare, of the outcomes of economic growth and expanding markets, and of the political effects of scientific knowledge, we live in a world that is so diverse that we may increasingly feel less than certain of our place in and understanding of that world. In the diverse and complex natural and social world that has been traced in the chapters in this book, we would expect a problem with any account of that world which gave the impression that the world behaved in straightforward ways.

So, to take an example from our understanding of human health, it is often unclear why some people develop particular diseases, like cancers. Who do we blame when things go wrong like this? In the past we might have blamed a god or just fate. Now we look to employers, polluters, regulators, food manufacturers, the health service, or more broadly the general production system, capitalism and so on. Governments sometimes ask us to blame only ourselves (see Chapter 2). What is apparent is that once we have mixed up the social and the natural, blame does not sit comfortably in inner nature, outer nature or in many of our social institutions. This is one reason for the protracted battles involving various experts who will try to convince you that 'their' department was not responsible or that we should be looking at so-and-so for an explanation. All of this buck-passing and finger-pointing is of course the stuff on which the media thrive, and so we are all increasingly drawn into a world where counter-claim succeeds claim, and precedes another claim. As we are drawn in, so we start to catch glimpses of what it might be like to live in a risk society (see Chapters 2 and 4).

As social scientists we can try to work with, rather than ignore, diversity and uncertainty. In Chapter 4, Steve Hinchliffe suggested through the BSE example that such diversity can make us suspicious of overly simplistic accounts of the social and natural world. We can be critical of those people who claim undue certainty. But we can also use some powerful social science techniques to counter the claims of people who would use the idea of diversity and uncertainty to obscure their role in the making of events. Statistics, models and critical reading of texts and arguments are all part of the social scientists' toolkit. They allow us to build up complex accounts of society at the same time as affording a view of social and natural processes that allows us to be aware of the uneven distribution of power in society. As the authors of Chapter 3 demonstrated, it is sometimes useful to construct models of the world in order to understand some of the ways in which processes operate. Through their market model, Sue Himmelweit and Roberto Simonetti provide us with the tools to understand some of the important relationships that make a market work. In doing so, we start to understand some of the means by which markets affect distributions of costs and benefits. As the authors make clear, whilst we should never forget the limitations of the model, its understandings do help us to think in sophisticated ways about the necessary market or non-market policies for dealing with environmental degradation. It is important to emphasize the way their method works by first of all simplifying the world (the basis of the model) and then making the model progressively more complex. This can be contrasted with the ways in which politicians have used laboratory science, which were critiqued by Steve Hinchliffe in Chapter 4. In this case, the simplifications of the laboratory were treated too readily as the 'truth' and not enough care was taken when the model of disease and risk was to be used in a more complex natural and social world. In short, we constantly need to check that our models and the knowledge that we produce are relevant to the diverse and uncertain world in which we live.

Knowledge and knowing

Throughout the chapters in this book we have been sketching a world that is constituted from mixtures of social and natural matters. We have also tended to highlight the importance of *interrelationships* between nature and society as a way of explaining issues as diverse as intelligence, health, risk and economies. So health is a matter of social and natural inheritance (genes and class, bodies and cultures). Economies work by setting up particular relationships between society (internal) and nature (largely external). If we accept this version of the world (and it should be noted that it is far from being uncontested), then this will have effects on the ways in which we need to engage with the world. In other words, if the natural and social worlds are no longer best seen as separate matters, then this poses some challenges to our ways of understanding the world, our theories and our methods.

The first challenge is that we need to be able develop ways of seeing the world that refuse to purify that world into social units. Thus, economists need to be wary of those economic models (like the dominant neo-classical model) that tend to ignore environmental degradation. As we saw in Chapter 3, as soon as we relax the assumptions of the model, markets become much more than relationships between producers and consumers. Therefore, other economists have attempted to build new models, a task that has led to the establishment of new sub-disciplines (including environmental and ecological economics).

The second challenge is that social scientists need to be ready to take on those who would have us believe that the world is reducible to natural units. Throughout this book, the authors have largely agreed that we cannot understand human behaviour, intelligence, health, economy or risk by referring *solely* to the internal physical or chemical properties of a substance. We have already made this argument for genes and health in this Afterword, so I will finish by reiterating the point on risk that was presented in Chapter 4. To understand the hazard or danger of a substance it is important not only to understand something of its chemical, biological and physical attributes, it is also vital to understand its social life – where it gets used, what people do with it, what they want from it, if the users know the consequences of misuse, if the dangers are explained, how often it is used.

Without the two sides of the coin, the natural *and* the social, we will end up with inappropriate knowledge. To say that something is safe on the basis of chemical properties alone is to invite disaster (partly because a grossly simplified social world *is* being assumed for any such statement). As social scientists, we need to be mindful of how to build up evidence that will allow us to understand both the social and the natural. In order to do so, we will need to broaden our understanding of who is the expert and what counts as knowledge in our societies. This and other challenges are taken up by **Hughes and Fergusson (2000)**, who look in more detail at the ways in which social institutions shape and are being reshaped in contemporary society

References

Hughes, G. and Fergusson, R. (eds) (2000) *Ordering Lives: Family, Work and Welfare,* London, Routledge/The Open University.

Latour, B. (1993) *We Have Never Been Modern*, London and New York, Harvester Wheatsheaf.

Rose, S. (1997) *Lifelines: Biology, Freedom, Determinism*, Harmondsworth, Penguin.

Acknowledgements

Grateful acknowledgement is made to the following sources for permission to reproduce material in this book.

Introduction

Figure 2: Ian Clifford Lott/Environmental Images.

Chapter 1

Figure 1.1: English Heritage Photographic Library; Figures 1.2 and 1.3: From 'Sexual strategies theory: an evolutionary perspective on human mating', by D M. Buss and D.P. Schmitt, 1993, *Psychological Review*, 100, pp.219 and 224. Copyright © 1993 by the American Psychological Association. Reprinted with permission; Figures 1.4, 1.5 and 1.6: Eysenck, H.J. (1953) *Uses and Abuses of Psychology*, pp.43, 46 and 47–8. Penguin Books, London. Copyright © H.J. Eysenck 1953. Reproduced by permission of Penguin Books Ltd; Figure 1.7: unable to trace source; Figure 1.13: Donaldson, M. (1978) *Children's Minds*, HarperCollins Publishers Ltd.

Chapter 2

Figures

Figure 2.1: © Health Education Authority. Reproduced with permission; Figure 2.2: Hellier Mason/Still Pictures; Figure 2.3: Mary Evans Picture Library; Figure 2 4: Science Museum/Science and Society Picture Library; Figure 2.5: Cover from Hindley, J. and King, C. (1975) *How Your Body Works*, Usborne Publishing Ltd, London, reproduced with permission; Figure 2.6: Whitehead, M. (1992) 'The health divide', in *Inequalities in Health*, Penguin Books Ltd, London, p.230, © Margaret Whitehead, 1988, 1992. Reproduced by permission of Penguin Books Ltd.

Table

Table 2.1: *Mortality Statistics, Perinatal and Infant: Social and Biological Factors, 1978–79 and 199*, (1995) Office for National Statistics. © Crown Copyright is reproduced with the permission of the Controller of Her Majesty's Stationery Office.

Chapter 3

Figures

Figure 3.1: adapted from MacGillivray, A. (1994) *Environmental Measures: Indicators for the UK Environment*, New Economics Foundation; Figure 3.3:

Mike Levers/Open University; Figure 3.4: A. Maslennikov/Still Pictures; Figure 3.5: Mark Edwards/Still Pictures.

Cartoons

p.101: © Dickinson/Punch; p. 111: © Albert/Punch.

Chapter 4

Text

Elliott, L. (1998) 'A tale of two catastrophies', *The Guardian*, 7 November 1998, © Guardian Newspapers Ltd.

Figures

Figure 4.1: Stan Gamester/Environmental Images; Figure 4.2: Northampton Press Agency; Figure 4.3: Nick Cobbing/Still Pictures; Figure 4.4: Bell, S. (1988) *If. ... Breezes In*, Methuen, © Steve Bell 1987 & 1988; Figure 4.5 (left): Mitch Jacobson/Associated Press; Figure 4.5 (right): Oswaldo Rivas/Popperfoto; Figure 4.6a (top): Jorgen Schytte/Still Pictures; Figures 4.6a (bottom), 4.6b and 4.8: Nigel Dickinson/Still Pictures; Figure 4.7: Bert Hardy/Hulton Getty Picture Collection; Figure 4.9: Pete Addis/Environmental Images.

Cover

Image copyright © 1996 PhotoDisc, Inc.

Every effort has been made to trace all copyright owners, but if any has been inadvertently overlooked, the publishers will be pleased to make the necessary arrangements at the first opportunity.

Index

acid rain 102
acupuncture 57, 62, 73
adoption studies of intelligence 26
and selective placement 27
age of mothers, and infant mortality
rates 54–5
agency, and structure 151, 156–7
air
as a public good 105
as a shared resource 81
air pollution, and health 46, 63, 69
Allen, J. 150
allopathy 58
alternative therapies 57–8
see also complementary health
movement
Angier, N. 17
animal experiments
and assessments of risks to human
health 146–7
and the BSE crisis 143–4
animal welfare, and meat production
138
aspirin, and heart attacks 52
asthma, explanations and
management of 44, 46, 71–3

babies
designer babies 9
infant mortality and social class
53–5
banking crisis (Wall Street) 128, 129,
130, 131, 132
bar charts, interpreting 15
Beck, Ulrich 136, 152
beef eating, and the BSE crisis 137–8,
140, 144
biology
and health 47, 49–50, 51–2, 63
and human nature 8–9
see also inner nature
'The Black Report' (government
report) 53
body, as a machine 50
body–mind relations
and health and illness 48–50, 61
holistic approach to 59–61
Bowlby, John 29, 30
British Medical Association 51, 58
Bruner, Jeremy, *Child's Talk* 39

BSE (Bovine Spongiform
Encephalopathy) crisis 119, 137–51,
152, 158
and beef eating 137–8, 140, 144–5
experts' views 141–4
and feelings of mistrust 148–50
and the risk society 139–40
and structure of feeling 146, 150,
151
Burt, Cyril 30
Buss, David, on sexual selection
15–17

Central American crisis (Hurricane
Mitch) 128, 129, 130, 131–5, 137,
151, 152
CFC gases 83
Chernobyl disaster 82
Child's Talk (Bruner) 39
child development 28–40, 118
cognitive processes of 29, 30–6
nature and nurture in 28–9
children, and power in the market
109
chimpanzees, and DNA differences
with humans 14, 18
chiropractic therapy 57, 58
CJD (Creutzfeldt-Jakob Disease) 139,
142, 143
climate
identifying causes of floods
119–26
as a shared resource 81
cloning 1–2, 19, 41, 155
cognitive development
genetic and social inheritance 4
Piaget's theory of 39–6, 40
criticism of 38–9
collective monologue in children 31
commodity exchange, and markets
86–7, 88
communities, and health promotion
63–4
complementary health movement
57–62
and asthma 72–3
holistic 59–60, 61
and physiological changes 61–2
reasons for 58–9
concrete operations 36

conservation experiments 34–6,
36–7
consumers
and the environment 106
and externalities of environmental
degradation 101
and the interests of future
generations 105–6
and market prices 92, 94, 95, 96,
97, 100
multiple sales 98, 99
surplus 93
and the neoclassical theory of
markets 88–9
sovereignty of 100
see also food
consumption, and lifestyle 65
contested concepts, health and
disease as 48
convergers 23
core and periphery, and world
financial markets 130
correlation, and IQ scores 24–5
criminality, and genetic inheritance 8

Darwin, Charles 10, 11–13, 19
and neo-Darwinism 13–14, 15–17,
18
Dealler, Dr Stephen 142, 143
deaths
from childhood illnesses 47
infant mortality rates 53–5
neonatal (perinatal) death rates
47, 53, 54–5
debt repayments, and the Central
American crisis 132
Descartes, René 48–9, 50
designer babies 9
diet, and health 63, 137–8
diseases
and genetic screening 69–70
see also health and illness
divergers 23
diversity, and uncertainty 157–8
see also uncertainty
DNA (deoxyribonucleic acid) 8, 13
differences between
chimpanzees and humans
14, 18
see also genes

doctors
  and the medical model of illness
    48, 49–50
  and New Public Health 69
Donaldson, Margaret, policeman
  experiment in *Children's Minds*
  37–8
drugs, and the complementary
  health movement 58, 59
dualism, of mind and body 48–50,
  61

economic agents 87–8
economic growth
  and environmental degradation
    82, 84–5
  in Japan, the UK and the USA
    82–3
egocentric speech in children 30–1
El Niño 120–1, 123, 126
environment
  and evolution 11–12, 13–14
  and green consciousness 81–2
  nature and society 2–4, 5, 80–5,
    155
  and non-human shared resources
    80–1
  problems of valuing the
    environment 109–10
  see also natural hazards; outer
    nature
Environmental Agency, on the causes
  of flooding 121–3, 126
environmental degradation
  and economic growth 82, 84–5
  externalities of 101–7
    distributional implications of
    108
  and future generations 105–6,
    111
  and power in the market 108–9
  reasons for 83–5
  role of markets in 5, 84–5, 106–7,
    158, 159
  value on loss through 110
  see also pollution
environmental disasters
  and human nature 8
  large-scale 82
  see also natural hazards
environmental risk 119–51
  and food scares 119
  and natural hazards 119–35
  reduction 71
European Union, fishing quotas 105

evolution 9, 10–18
  and the environment 11–12, 13–14
  and genes 13–18
exchange, and markets 86–7, 88
exhaustible resources 103–5
experts, and the BSE crisis 141–4
externalities
  and environmental degradation
    101–7
    distributional implications of
    108, 111

feminist critiques of science
  and laboratory science 148
  and neo-Darwinism 14
Fergusson, R. 152, 159
financial crisis (Wall Street) 128, 129,
  130, 131, 132
fish stocks 80
  and fishing quotas 105
  social costs of overfishing 103
fixed notions of identity 8–9
floods, identifying causes of 119–26
food
  and environmental risk 119,
    136–51
  genetically-modified 46, 69, 150
  and health risks 68–9
  and lifestyle choices 66
  see also consumers
formal operations stage of child
  development 33

Galton, Francis 19, 20
gender, and criteria for selecting a
  mate 15–18
  see also sex differences
gene therapy 41
genes
  and disease 46
  genetic differences and evolution
    13–18
  and human nature 8, 9, 40
  properties of 14
  structure and agency 156
genetic inheritance
  and adoption studies 26, 27
  and child development 28–9
  and individual differences 8, 9–10,
    19–20, 27–8
  intelligence and cognitive
    development 4
  interactive explanations of 14–15,
    25
  and twin studies 20–5, 26–8

genetic screening 69–70
genetically-modified food 46, 69, 150
geographies
  of natural events 128, 133
  of vulnerability and vulnerability
    production 132–5
Giddens, Anthony, on lifestyle 64–5
global warming 69, 81
Gove, J. 8
governments
  and the BSE crisis 140, 141–3,
    144–5, 146, 150
  and environmental issues 81, 83
  and uncertainty and diversity
    157–8
GPD (Gross Domestic Product), in
  Japan, the UK and the USA 82, 83
green consciousness, emergence
  of 81–2
greenhouse gases, effects on
  health 69
Greenpeace 81
Gummer, John 141, 143

'The Health Divide' (government
  report) 53
health and illness 4–5, 44–77, 118, 159
  and asthma 44, 46, 71–3
  and the complementary health
    movement 57–62, 72–3
  medical conceptions of 48–52, 61,
    72
  New Public Health model of
    62–71, 73
  social explanations of 53–7, 72
  structure and agency in 157
health promotion 44–6, 63–4
  and lifestyle choices 64–7
  and risk 67–71, 73
health services
  expenditure on 46
  National Health Service 46–7, 52,
    58
heart attacks, medical model of 51–2
histories of natural events 127–8, 133
HIV positive testing, and genetic
  screening 70
holistic approach to health and illness
  59–60, 61
homeopathy 57, 58
housing, and health 56, 63, 72
Hudson, Liam 23
Hughes, G. 152, 159
human cloning 1–2, 19, 41, 155
Human Genome Project 69

human nature 4, 8–41, 118
and child development 28–40, 118
and evolution 9, 10–18
and intelligence 19–28
Hurricane Mitch *see* Central American crisis

identical twins 9, 19, 28
and IQ scores 24–5
and selective placement for adoption 27
identity
fixed notions of 8–9
and lifestyle 64–5
illness *see* health and illness
individual differences 19–28
in child development 39
and genetic inheritance 8, 9–10, 19–20, 27–8
and studies of twins 9, 19, 20–5
individuals
food safety and risk calculation 145–6, 151
and the medical model of illness 52
responsibility for health 63, 67, 69
and lifestyle choices 4, 63, 64–7, 68, 70
and risk 63, 69, 70–1
infant mortality rates, and social class 53–5
inner nature 1, 4–5, 9, 10, 18, 137
and the BSE crisis 138–9
structure and agency 156–7
see also biology
intelligence 19–28
adoption studies of 26, 27
genetic and social inheritance 4, 9, 18, 19–20, 40
studies of intellectual development 36–40
stages of 32–6
twin studies of 9, 19, 20–5
criticisms of 26–8
'invisible elbow' model of markets 106–7
controlling 107–12
IQ tests 41
and twin studies 20–5, 27, 28
IQs (intelligence quotients) 20
and adoption studies 26

Jacobs, Michael 106
Japan, economic growth 82, 83

knowledge and knowing 158–9

Lacey, Professor Richard 142, 143
Lalonde, Marc 62
landscapes, natural and social 2–3, 155
language, and socialization 38–9
Latour, Bruno 3
life expectancy
increase in 47
and social class 53, 55–6
lifestyle choices, and health 4, 63, 64–7, 68, 69
Light, Paul 36

Mae-Wan Ho 14
market adjustments 5
market economies 84–5, 86
market forces 84
markets 86–115, 118, 155, 158
defining 86–7
and economic agents 87–8
and environmental degradation 5, 84–5, 100–7, 110–12, 158, 159
and externalities 100–7, 111
and the interests of future generations 105–6, 111
'invisible elbow' model of 106–7
controlling 107–12
'invisible hand' model of 88, 90, 99, 100, 106, 107
modelling 90–2
with multiple sales 98–100
neoclassical model of 88–90, 91, 100, 110–11, 112, 159
power in the market 108–9
and the price mechanism 89–90, 91, 92–100, 106, 112
Stage 1 (no market) 93–5
Stage 2 (introducing the market) 95–6
Stage 3 (equilibrium prices) 96–7, 98–9, 99–100
and property rights 87, 88, 103, 107, 108, 110, 112
social costs and benefits of 101–2, 103–4
structure and agency in 157
and vulnerability 129–30
Marx, Karl 10
maternal deprivation, Bowlby's studies of 29
media
and the complementary health movement 57

and genetic screening 70
and health promotion 44, 63, 69
and lifestyle choices 65–6
Meldrum, Keith 141, 142–3
middle classes, and health promotion 68
mind *see* body–mind relations
mobile telephone use, risks of compared with eating beef 145
models
defining 90–1
of markets 90–100, 158
how prices are formed 92–100, 112
'invisible elbow' 106–7
'invisible hand' 88, 90, 99, 100, 106, 107
neoclassical 88–90, 91, 100, 110–11, 112
of risk 148
Mooney, G. 8
mortality rates, and social class 53–6
motherese (mother–child speech) 39
multinational corporations, and the Central American crisis 131–2

National Health Service 46–7, 52, 58
national parks 2–3
National Trust 87
natural hazards 119–35, 157, 159
attributing blame for 121–7, 157–8
denial of responsibility for 137
nature and society 123–6, 137, 151
and uneven geographies of risk 128–35
and vulnerability 127–8, 137
see also environmental disasters
natural resources
exhaustible 103–5
shared 80–1, 108
natural selection 12
naturalistic experiments, in studies of child development 34–8
nature and society
and the BSE crisis 146
and the mind–body dualism 50
and natural disasters 123–6, 137, 151
interrelationship 1–5, 118–19, 155–6, 159
limitations of separating 118–19, 127, 147–8, 151–2
and risk 137, 147–8, 150

see also inner nature; outer nature; purified view of nature and society
negative externalities
for future generations 105–6
and markets 101–2, 103, 104
neo-Darwinists
and genes 13–14
and sexual selection 15–17, 18
neoclassical model of markets 88–90, 91, 100, 110–11, 112, 159
networked computers, and financial markets 87
New Public Health 62–71
and asthma 73
non-identical twins 9, 20
and IQ scores 24–5

open-ended tests 23
operational stage of child development 33
organic food 68, 69
osteopathy 57
Ottawa Charter for Health Promotion 63
outer nature 1, 137
and the BSE crisis 138–9
structure and agency in 157
see also environment

Pasteur, Louis 49
periphery and core, and world financial markets 130
Piaget, Jean
theory of cognitive development 30–6
criticisms of 38–9
pollution
acid rain 102
air pollution 46, 63, 69
and green taxes and subsidies 105, 107, 108, 109–10, 111, 112
and power in the market 108, 109
see also environmental degradation
positive externalities, and markets 101
poverty
and power in the market 109
and vulnerability to natural hazards 127, 128
power in the market 108–9
pre-operational stage of child development 33

precautionary approach to risks 143
Prevention and Health: Everybody's Business (Department of Health and Social Security) 63
price mechanism
and the market 89–90, 91, 92–100, 106, 112
Stage 1 (no market) 93–5
Stage 2 (introducing the market) 95–6
Stage 3 (equilibrium prices) 96–7, 98–9, 99–100
private costs and benefits, of market transactions 101, 107
private ownership
of exhaustible resources 103–4
and property rights 87, 88, 103, 107, 108, 110
and public goods 105
producers
and externalities of environmental degradation 101–1
and market prices 92, 94, 95, 96, 97, 98, 100
multiple sales 98, 99
surplus 93
property rights
and markets 87, 88, 103, 107, 108, 110, 112
and public goods 105
public awareness of risk 136
and the BSE crisis 140
public goods 105
purified view of nature and society 1, 3–4, 118, 123, 155
and laboratory tests 147, 148

resources *see* natural resources
risk
defining 119
factors associated with health 68–71, 73
health and illness 4–5
living with 136–7
and the BSE crisis 137–51
meanings of 67–8
nature and society 4, 5, 156
precautionary approach to 143
rationalities and cultures of 144–51
see also environmental risk
risk management, uneven vulnerability through 130–5, 137
risk society
and the BSE crisis 139–40, 145

characteristics of 136
and nature–society relations 136–7
and uncertainty 158
Rose, Hilary 9
Rose, Steven 156

science
and the BSE crisis 141, 142–4, 148–50
and the complementary health movement 61–2
and the medical model of illness 51
and risk assessment 146–50
see also animal experiments
self-discipline, and health 67, 69
sensori-motor stage of child development 33
sex differences, and genetic explanations of evolution 15–18
shared resources, and the environment 80–1, 108
skin cancer 69
Smith, Adam 87, 90
The Wealth of Nations 88
and the 'invisible hand' 88, 90, 99, 100, 106, 107
SMR (standardized mortality ratio) 55
Snowdonia National Park 2–3
social class
defining 53–4
and health and illness 53–6
and health promotion 68
social costs and benefits, of market transactions 101–2, 103–4, 107
social intelligence 23
social order/disorder, and natural disasters 123–6
social ownership
of exhaustible resources 105
and public goods 105
social science
and complex causes 126, 127
as a form of investigation 10, 40, 122
and living with risk 146
society and nature
and the BSE crisis 146
and the mind–body dualism 50
and natural disasters 123–6, 137, 151
interrelationship 1–5, 118–19, 155–6, 159
limitations of separating 118–19, 127, 147–8, 151–2
and risk 137, 147–8, 150

see also inner nature; outer nature;
purified view of nature and
society
species being 10
and environmental change
11–12
and genes 13
speech
egocentric speech and collective
monologue 30–1
socialization of actions through 38
stethoscopes, and the medical model
49
stress, and illness 46
structure, and agency 151,
156–7
structure of feeling, and the BSE
crisis 146, 150, 151

Taoist Yin-Yang symbol 60, 62
taxation, green taxes 105, 107, 108,
109, 111, 112

trust
declining
and the BSE crisis
148–50
and the risk society 136,
140
twin studies of intelligence 9, 19,
20–5
criticisms of 26–8

uncertainty
and the BSE crisis 143–4
and diversity 157–8
and living with risk 136
and models of risk 148
nature and society 4, 156
Union Carbide gas leak (Bhopal)
82
unit costs, and market prices 92,
94, 96, 97, 98
United Kingdom, economic
growth 82, 83

United States of America, economic
growth 82, 83

vaccination programmes 51
verbal tests 23
vulnerability
defining 127
and markets 129–30
and natural hazards 127–8, 137,
157
uneven, through risk
management 130–5

Wall Street crisis 128, 129, 130,
131, 132
water as a shared resource 81
Watt, S. 8
The Wealth of Nations (Smith)
88
Woodward, K. 9, 127
World Health Organization 69